What readers are saying about Gary W. Kuhne's first book—

The Dynamics of Personal Follow-up

"I believe it is the best expression of the one-on-one principle of discipleship I have ever read."
>—Harry D. Williams
>>Director of the Department
>>of Evangelism
>>Southern Baptist Convention

". . . a long-needed book. . . . Here is the greatest strength of the book—explicit instructions in techniques."
>—Glenn Anderson
>>in *The Standard*

". . . a book that wants to plant in your mind a concern for the new convert. That you will nurture him in the faith; feeding him with the milk, before you feed him the meat."
>—Samuel Sterrett
>>*Blue Banner Faith and Life*
>>Quarterly Bible Study Journal

The Dynamics of Discipleship Training

Being and Producing
Spiritual Leaders

Gary W. Kuhne

Zondervan Publishing House
Grand Rapids, Michigan

THE DYNAMICS OF DISCIPLESHIP TRAINING
© 1978 by The Zondervan Corporation
Grand Rapids, Michigan

Zondervan Books are published by Zondervan
Publishing House, 1415 Lake Drive, S.E.,
Grand Rapids, Michigan 49506

Library of Congress Cataloging in Publication Data

Kuhne, Gary W
    The dynamics of discipleship training.

    Companion volume to the author's The dynamics of personal follow-up.
    1. Christian life—1960—   I. Title.
BV4501.2.K77   248'.42   77-12651

ISBN 0-310-26961-X

Printed in the United States of America

89   90 / 16   15   14   13

Contents

Acknowledgments

I would like to admit the debt I owe to the many people who helped contribute to this book directly or indirectly. I want to thank my fellow staff, past and present, with Campus and Lay Mobilization for their role in developing the practicality of this book; for without their years of field testing of the concepts herein developed, and their vigorous discussions on the applications, this book would have been sterile and academic.

Many thanks to my brother Mark and Lana Bower, who spent innumerable hours over a typewriter putting data into useable form.

Also I want to give special acknowledgment to my wife, Karen. Her typing of the final manuscript was a long job, which she did without complaining. Her love for me was long-suffering as I spent hours rightfully hers in the writing of this volume. As in so many other cases, a godly wife is the primary reason anything of any import gets accomplished. This book is no exception, and thus it is to my wife that I dedicate this book.

Introduction

In the period of time since the publication of my first book, *The Dynamics of Personal Follow-up*, I have been contacted by many people who found the ideas offered there particularly helpful in their personal ministries. I am gratified at the apparent usefulness of that book and the way God has blessed it. Almost without exception, however, these people have requested further help in developing their ministries.

My previous book, although developing the concept of a disciple-building ministry, focused primarily on the work of ministry to new Christians. Yet in the production of disciples, personal follow-up is but the first step. How do we move from the point of having stabilized a new Christian in his faith to the point of having a truly multiplying, productive disciple? It is the answer to this question that this book is addressed.

I conceive of this to be as a companion volume to my first book. It is my prayer that together they will provide the necessary training and stimulus to the Christian community at large to hasten the time of the fulfillment of the Great Commission. May God richly bless you, the reader, as you seek to implement the joy-filled task of reproducing yourself in others through the ministry of discipleship training.

1

Gaining the Vision of Disciple-Making

> And the things you have heard me say in the presence of many witnesses entrust to reliable men who will also be qualified to teach others (2 Tim. 2:2).

Just prior to His ascension into heaven, Jesus Christ gave His small band of faithful followers one of the most important commands of His earthly ministry. The effective fulfillment of this command would determine the success of growth of the kingdom of God in this age. The command, often referred to as the Great Commission, is found in Matthew 28:18-20:

> Then Jesus came to them and said, "All authority in heaven and on earth has been given to me. Therefore go and make disciples of all nations, baptizing them in the name of the Father and of the Son and of the Holy Spirit, and teaching them to obey everything I have commanded you. And surely I will be with you always, to the very end of the age."

An examination of this command reveals some points

essential to our understanding of the Great Commission. The focal point of the command is that the main goal is to make disciples. This seemingly obvious truth has some important implications to any Christian sincerely desiring to fully obey his Lord.

First, the command to evangelize is nowhere given. Yet evangelism is the usual emphasis derived from this passage. While it is not incorrect to teach this, since the first step in making a disciple is to win a person to Christ, it would be a terrible mistake to stop there and never go beyond the communication of the gospel. We are commanded to make disciples, not merely adherents, as the product of our ministries. By stating the command the way He did, Christ insured a perspective on ministry that went beyond the initial step of evangelism. Since we are a people addicted to shortcuts, such a precaution was necessary.

A second implication of Christ's command is that the means of achieving the Great Commission depends not so much on better techniques and greater technology, but rather on the development of committed people. This multiplication of disciples is commanded because people are reached for Christ most effectively through other people. The reality of the gospel, of new life in Christ, is not so much written about as lived. The divine plan for saturating our world with the gospel is through the multiplication of people who are committed to the lordship of Christ in all aspects of their lives.

At first glance it seems strange that the Lord would choose this plan. Human beings are so much less reliable than machines and much more prone to error. It would seem that there are too many variables in man to make it wise to stake something as crucial as the Great Commission on his faithfulness. Yet this is exactly what God has done — with one important addition: He is *with* us in this work. The fulfillment of the Great Commission is not a self-effort project. The authority and power of heaven are at our disposal in the accomplishing of this divine command. Through the enabling power of the Holy Spirit, the impossible becomes possible. And it is at this point that the strategy begins to make sense. The clearest way to see the reality of the gospel message is to see the mature believer demonstrating the fruits of the Spirit in his life and in his relationships with non-Christians. In fact, this was part of the value of the incarnation of Christ — we were able to see the divine in human terms we could comprehend. The assurance of God *with* us makes all the difference.

At this point there is profit in defining the term *disciple* so you can gain a firmer grip on the implications of Matthew 28:18-20. The following is a definition of *disciple* that I believe to be quite complete and workable:

> A *disciple* is a Christian who is growing in conformity to Christ, is achieving fruit in evangelism, and is working in follow-up to conserve his fruit.

This is the type of individual we are commanded to develop around the world.

I vividly remember my confusion as a young Christian burdened with the need to work with new Christians and turn them into disciples. There were so many questions floating around in my head that no one seemed able to answer: Was I mature enough to help someone else to grow in Christ? What does it mean to grow in Christ anyway? What exactly is a disciple? How long must I work with someone to make him into a disciple? Who would disciple me?

I found out that many others were asking the same questions. I also discovered that there were some excellent books written to answer some of them. Several books were written to answer the question, What is a disciple?[1] Others had been written to determine the methods followed by

13

Christ in making His disciples.[2] Yet none of these books gave me practical, step-by-step guidelines to actually carry out a personal ministry of disciple-building. I needed training on how to *build* as well as *be* a disciple. My ministry in the years since that time have been spent seeking to develop transferable concepts in the work of building disciples. This book reflects my findings.

Returning to the definition of a disciple as previously given, I belive it is important to add some meat to the bare bones of the definition. Without a clear, comprehensive picture of what we are trying to achieve when building a disciple, we will never know when we have achieved our goals. As you read through this book, you should gain a better sense of what the right goals are, not only because I define them, but also because you will see what you are to be like in your own growth in Christ to produce disciples, thus gaining a personal awareness of the end results.

Let me hasten to add at this early stage that true discipleship is a lifelong process. We never reach an arbitrary point where we can feel we have "arrived." When I talk about building disciples, I do not mean totally mature individuals, but rather bringing a person to the point where the necessary disciplines of Christian living have been built into him so the lifelong process of maturing can reasonably be expected to continue in his own Christian experience. That a person never arrives at a point where discipling stops is seen in Paul's admission in his letter to the Christians at Philippi:

> Not that I have already obtained this or am already perfect; but I press on to make it my own . . . (Phil. 3:12).

This book on building disciples uses a more limited concept when employing the term *disciple*. As previously intimated, the concept I am using could be summarized by saying a person becomes a disciple when he becomes stabilized in the faith, has an ongoing commitment to the lordship of Christ, and has developed the basic disciplines of Christian living and service so that the lifelong maturing process is guaranteed, at least as much as is humanly possible. This somewhat expanded definition is a good place to begin the discussion of discipleship training and immediately identifies certain inherent needs in this type of ministry.

First, to be growing in Christ, a Christian must meet certain conditions. He must have a basic understanding of his faith, have a regular devotional time, be involved in good fellowship, and be instructed in the Word of God. Second, the Christian desiring to grow in Christ must be obeying and applying what God has commanded him through the Bible. Such a life style of obedience is basic to true discipleship. Third, he must receive regular training in the practical aspects of outreach and ministry so that he can be fruitful and conserve that fruit.

THE VISION FOR MULTIPLYING

The goal of our disciple-building work could be summarized in another way by saying we are seeking to produce a transferer, or a teacher. A true disciple is a teacher in the sense that he is involved in communicating the truths of God's Word to others on a personal level. The Great Commission clearly includes this idea of teaching and building teachers. It is therefore imperative that we be working to produce individuals capable of teaching others if we are to have the process of disciple-building continue beyond ourselves. Hebrews 5:11,12 is a classic passage which shows that the production of teachers is the legitimate goal of our disciple-building, and something is seriously wrong when this is not achieved.

> We have much to say about this, but it is hard to explain because you are slow to learn. In fact, though *by this time you ought to be teachers,* you need someone to teach you the elementary truths of God's Word all over again.

15

When I saw that I should be working toward reproduction in my training ministry was perhaps one of the most important lessons the Lord has ever taught me. Prior to realizing this, my personal ministry was geared to stabilizing believers. The frustration in this effort was that I never found any help from those I stabilized in my ongoing ministry to others. I knew something was wrong, but I couldn't see it until I read 2 Timothy 2:2 and meditated on its implications. This passage underscores the method of ministry employed by Paul. It involved not only teaching, but also training to enable those he worked with to minister to others, to become teachers themselves.

> And the things what you have heard me say in the presence of many witnesses entrust (teach) to reliable men who will also be qualified to teach others.

Such a ministry is summarized by the concept of multiplication. One disciple must be developing other disciples, who in turn can develop other disciples. It is the concept of multiplication which underlies the purpose of this book. The production of multiplying disciples is the only way to effectively fulfill the Great Commission, and multiplying disciples are best produced through discipleship training. A few definitions are in order at this point. The following are terms that will be used throughout the remainder of this book.

> *Discipleship training* is the spiritual work of developing spiritual maturity and spiritual reproductiveness in the life of a Christian.
>
> *Multiplication* is third-generation discipleship training.
>
> A *multiplier* is a disciple who is training his spiritual children to reproduce themselves.

For multiplication to occur, a mature Christian must make a conscious decision to work in discipleship training with new Christians. Until I actually came to the point of doing this, I did not see a growing fruitfulness from my ministry.

At this point a review of the multiplication process is in order. There are a number of excellent books developing this concept which should be read for a more complete picture.[3] Multiplication is a process that goes through four distinct phases. Starting from the ministry of evangelism, these phases show how multiplication causes the progressive fulfillment of the Great Commission command.

Phase one is simply to evangelize. This phase focuses on our personally sharing of our faith with the non-Christian world around us. As already pointed out, this is an activity inherent in the Great Commission. There is no option here for the committed Christian. Although the method of sharing may vary, the command is universal in application. When fruit results from your evangelism, you are ready to begin phase two of the multiplication process.

Phase two of the multiplication process is doing personal follow-up with the individual who has repented and believed in Christ as Savior. The need and method for this type of ministry I have developed at length in a previous book.[4] The stabilizing of new Christians is part of what must be done to fulfill the command of God previously examined. Once a Christian has been stabilized, you are ready to begin the third phase in the multiplication process.

Phase three is discipling the new Christian. The goal of this phase is to produce spiritual maturity and fruitfulness in ministry in the life of this Christian. This is the process the present volume addresses. Yet, for multiplication to actually occur, there is another phase that must take place. It is not enough to help a person to become a mature Christian or even fruitful in evangelism. The disciple you are developing must actually *be involved* in training others, in reproducing what he has learned in the lives of others.

Phase four occurs when the person with whom you are working actually succeeds in producing other disciples. This is when 2 Timothy 2:2 becomes a reality in your ministry. True multiplication only occurs when you have reached phase four. At this stage the person you are working with proves his faithfulness and commitment. The Great Commission is never really going to be fulfilled until multiplication is achieved.

To further prove the far-reaching effects of such an intensive ministry that multiplication requires, let's look at some statistics. Assume for a moment that you could stimulate and produce one truly multiplying disciple each year. I have personally found this to be possible (remember that I am referring to establishing in a Christian those characteristics necessary to assure a lifelong growing process). The following statistical study clearly shows the far-reaching effect of such an intensive, multiplying ministry. An evangelism contact figure is also given, based on an average of fifty contacts per year for each multiplying disciple.

Year One
> 1. Begin year 1 disciple (you)
> 2. End year 2 disciples (you, plus 1)
> 3. Evangelistic contacts: 50

Year Two
> 1. Begin year: 2 disciples
> 2. End year: 4 disciples
> 3. Evangelistic contacts: 100

Year Three
> 1. Begin year: 4 disciples
> 2. End year: 8 disciples
> 3. Evangelistic contacts: 200

Year Four

    1. Begin year: 8 disciples
    2. End year: 16 disciples
    3. Evangelistic contacts: 400

Year Five

    1. Begin year: 16 disciples
    2. End year: 32 disciples
    3. Evangelistic contacts: 800

Year Six

    1. Begin year: 32 disciples
    2. End year: 64 disciples
    3. Evangelistic contacts: 1,600

Continued at this rate, multiplication will produce 1,024 disciples and the annual confrontation with the gospel of over 25,000 people after ten years. This fantastic fruitfulness can result directly from your discipling ministry, even though you will only have worked with ten people over that decade. The only real variable is whether you work in such a way as to produce truly reproducing disciples. There is no question in my mind but that these results are achievable if we will carry out an intensive ministry, pouring our lives into others. Such a vision of multiplication is crucial for the average Christian and local church today. The manpower shortages and ineffective community penetration for the gospel could both be corrected by disciple-building to produce multiplication.

I know of a church that regularly registers more than fifty "decisions" for Christ each year through its various ministries. Yet no one is willing to work with the results of such evangelism. There has been an increase of only fifty in attendance over the past decade, and it is always the same faithful core doing all the work. When one of the faithful core is forced to leave the area because of work transfers, there is a major crisis in the church because there is no one to take his place. There is just no leadership development taking place. God's obvious blessings in evangelism are not being matched by growth because there are no conserving or building ministries taking place. The church is no closer to winning its community than it was a decade ago.

I am sure you have run into the following situation as often as I have. A group of deacons, or trustees, or some other committee in charge of the church's ministry, are standing around lamenting their problems. "If only we had more people as committed as Bill." "If only more people had the love for others Mary has." "If only we could get others to give as sacrificially as Tom." Does this sound familiar? The tragedy of such conversations is that they will still be echoing in church corridors twenty years from now unless the vision of discipling is caught. The best way for more Bills and Marys and Toms to come on the scene is for Bill and Mary and Tom to share their lives with others in discipling. Remember the promise of Luke 6:40:

> A disciple . . . when he is fully taught will be like his teacher (RSV).

Committed Christians must begin to reproduce themselves in others if the manpower problems of the kingdom are to be alleviated.

This book will focus on the data necessary for achieving phases three and four of the process of multiplication. By exploring principles, curriculum, and "how to's," I hope to show those who are reading how to reproduce themselves in the lives of others.

FINDING FAITHFUL MEN

A good place to begin our discussion of reproducing our life in others is to say that not everyone is ready to be involved in discipleship training. Disciple-building is not a one-way process, but rather requires joint participation between the discipler and disciple to prove effective. It will serve no purpose to meet and train someone who has no intention of reproducing such training in the lives of others. Multiplication can never occur without such reproduction occurring.

From the previous discussion of multiplication, there are certain demands that cannot be overlooked in such a ministry. Perhaps the most important is the requirement that you spend much time with one person to build them. You are making a conscious choice to restrict your other ministries and stake your future productivity on the faithful ministries of those whom you build. If the people you disciple don't carry on a similar ministry in the lives of other people, you will have nothing to show for your effort, at least not in the sense of multiplication. I hope you can sense the seriousness of the choice, or selection, to which I am referring. To make the wrong selection is to submit yourself to a fruitless and unrewarding ministry. Perhaps a personal example will better explain the reasons for my warnings.

Frank was a college freshman whom I had led to Christ. I began to go through a program of personal follow-up with him. He seemed hungry to know more about his faith, so I began to spend an increasing amount of time with him. Soon I reached a point where I needed to make a choice. He was well grounded in his faith, so any more work I did would be categorized as discipleship training. Should I continue into this type of ministry with Frank, or should I be content with just making sure he stays faithful to the Lord? There were a number of signs which began to indicate a lack of faithfulness in Frank. In spite of this, I decided to continue to work with him in discipleship training. I worked weekly with Frank for nearly a year. I poured precious time and energy into him during that time. What was the result? Nothing. Frank has yet to begin to work with anyone else. He is inconsistent in important areas of his spiritual life. Because he was not ready to be worked with, I accomplished nothing. As Hebrews 5:11,12 puts it, although Frank should have been a teacher (multiplier), he was still needing work on the first principles of God's Word.

Perhaps this example from my experience illustrates what I have come to believe is the single biggest obstacle to Christians continuing in a personal ministry such as disciple-building. This obstacle is discouragement. Discouragement stems from such negative experiences as the one I have just described. To have spent precious time and effort pouring oneself into another person and have that person not grow or prove fruitful is tremendously disheartening.

Finding faithful men to work with is an important criterion in disciple-building. In addition to 2 Timothy 2:2, examine the emphasis the Bible lays on this criterion in the following verses, which expand our understanding of faithfulness.

1. *Finding faithful men is difficult.*

   Many a man proclaims his own loyalty, but a *faithful man* who can find? (Prov. 20:6).

   ... However, when the Son of Man comes, will he find *faith* on the earth? (Luke 18:8).

2. *Faithfulness equals fruitfulness.*

   Parable of the Talents (Matt. 25:14–30).

3. *There is joy in finding faithful men.*

   Like the cold snow in the time of harvest is a *faithful* messenger to those who send him (Prov. 25:13).

   I have no greater joy than to hear that my children are living according to the truth (3 John 4).

These and other verses certainly stress the need for finding faithful, trustworthy men to work with. Are there objective criteria you can utilize for determining faithful men? The

Bible identifies several that should help you determine faithful prospects for discipleship training.

CRITERIA FOR FAITHFUL MEN

1. A Hunger for God's Word

First, search for those people who have a real hunger for God's Word. This usually reveals a desire for growth and increased knowledge of God, which are important characteristics of a disciple. Closely related to this is a commitment to the authority of the Word. The person doesn't pick and choose what to believe and act upon. The Word of God describes such an attitude in the following verses:

> Like newborn babies, crave pure spiritual milk [of the Word], so that by it you may grow up in your salvation (1 Peter 2:2).

> Thy words were found, and I ate them, and thy word became to me a joy and the delight of my heart (Jer. 15:16).

> My soul is feasted as with marrow and fat,
>   and my mouth praises thee with joyful lips,
> when I think of thee upon my bed,
>   and meditate on thee in the watches of the night (Ps. 63:5,6).

> My soul is consumed with longing
>   for thy ordinances at all times (Ps. 119:20).

How will this hunger be demonstrated? Let me relate several examples from my experience. One new Christian I worked with read the whole New Testament in the first few weeks after his conversion. Another had memorized the salvation verses by our first follow-up appointment. Another new Christian had read the entire Book of John after one week. This attitude clearly delineates who is faithful and who isn't. I have yet to find a fruitful Christian who doesn't hunger for the Word.

2. A Thirst for Holy Living

A second criterion in discovering faithful men is to look for those with a thirst for holy living. This thirst would generally be characterized by a sorrow for past sins and a real joy in righteousness. Such a person truly desires to live the type of life God wants him to. When a faithful person comes into the presence of God, his first reaction is dismay over his sinfulness. Certainly this was the response of Isaiah in his vision of God in Isaiah 6. The practical result of this dismay over sin is a desire for holiness. Is the person you hope to work with desiring to be the Christlike individual God intends him to be? The following Scriptures identify with desire:

> We can be sure we know him if we obey his commands (1 John 2:3).

> But just as he who called you is holy, so be holy in all you do; for it is written: "Be holy, because I am holy" (1 Peter 1:15,16).

> Create in me a clean heart, O God, and put a new and right spirit within me (Ps. 51:10).

How will this thirst be demonstrated? I remember one man who was in his twenties when saved. After a prayer meeting I saw tears running down his cheeks. He told me that while praying he became aware of God's true holiness and his own sinfulness. This caused him to appreciate anew his justification and motivated him for holy living. Similarly, a college student I worked with shared with me that he wanted to be as good as he once was bad. There is a hymn which explains this longing as well as anything I have read.

> Search me, O God, and know my heart today;
> Try me, O Savior, know my thoughts, I pray.
> See if there be some wicked way in me;
> Cleanse me from every sin and set me free.

I praise Thee, Lord, for cleansing me from sin;
Fulfill Thy Word and make me pure within.
Fill me with fire where once I burned with shame;
Grant my desire to magnify Thy name.

3. A Desire for Greater Knowledge of God

A third criterion for discovering faithful men is to look for those who desire to know God better. By this I mean a hungering for the relationship lost in the Fall and experientially only partially regained in salvation (though fully regained positionally). This hungering would be evidenced in a desire to meditate on God as He has revealed Himself in nature and in the Word. Although less tangible in objective terms of measurement, it is still an important criterion. The following verses identify this point:

As a hart longs for flowing streams,
so longs my soul for thee, O God.
My soul thirsts for God,
for the living God (Ps. 42:1,2).

O God, thou art my God, I seek thee,
my soul thirsts for thee;
my flesh faints for thee, as in a dry and
weary land where no water is (Ps. 63:1).

4. A Basic Commitment to the Lordship of Christ

In search to discover faithful men, one must look for a basic commitment to the lordship of Christ. Such a commitment, or submission, to the lordship of Christ would be evidenced in two ways. The first would be a willingness to be obedient to all that God commands in His Word. This means no picking and choosing what to obey, but rather striving to become obedient in all areas of life to which the Word of God addresses itself. It is so refreshing in my ministry to come across people whose problem is wondering *how* to become obedient, not *whether* they will become obedient.

The second aspect of Lordship is a willingness to allow God to lead us into His perfect will for our lives. This involves the major decisions of mission and mate, as well as the everyday decisions we have to face. Is the Christian you are working with willing to do and be whatever God wants? It is on this practical level that commitment makes a difference. The following verses clearly spell out this need:

> You shall love the LORD your God with all your heart, and with all your soul, and with all your might (Deut. 6:5).

> But seek first his kingdom and his righteousness, and all these things will be given to you as well (Matt. 6:33).

> Do not conform any longer to the pattern of this world, but be transformed by the renewing of your mind. Then you will be able to test and approve what God's will is — his good, pleasing and perfect will (Rom. 12:2).

5. A Desire to Be Used by God

A fifth test for determining faithful men is to look for those who have a desire to be used. Does that Christian you are working with really desire for God to use him? Does he echo Isaiah's "Here am I! Send me"? Only having a deep desire to be used will sufficiently motivate a person to consistency in outreach. The attitude you are looking for is an excitement at the possibility of being God's instrument to win or build up someone else. Examine Paul's attitude toward ministry as it is reflected in the following verses:

> I long to see you so that I may impart to you some spiritual gift to make you strong (Rom. 1:11).

> That is why I am *eager* to preach the gospel . . . (Rom. 1:15).

> For I want you to know how greatly I *strive* for you . . . (Col. 2:1 RSV).

One very practical way to demonstrate a desire to be used is to seek out all the training available to you for effectiveness in ministry. In addition to training programs, a personal study program would be in order. Read and digest some of the many good books available on the topic of evangelism. By such activities you prove that you do indeed have a burden in this area. It is doing, not discussing, that proves your desire. Important as good preparation is, it never will achieve anything without actually going out and doing evangelism and other aspects of ministry.

A student I worked with several years ago had a great burden for the lost and really desired to be used to reach them. He literally pumped me dry of information on how to witness. Whenever we got together, he would have scores of questions to ask relating to some dimension of outreach. These questions grew out of field experience, not vain discussions with other Christians. His desire to be used was evidenced in this practical way. This is what we are looking for when seeking faithful men.

6. A Love for People

A sixth criterion in discovering faithful men is to find those who have a real love for people. This is closely aligned with the previous criterion of desire to be used. I am talking about having a heart for people. A person who has no heart for others will seldom prove to be faithful in the ministry. The heartfelt burden for people's salvation and growth is basic to true effectiveness. Notice this emphasis in the following verses:

> For the *love* of Christ controls us . . . (2 Cor. 5:14 RSV).

> For God is my witness, how I *yearn* for you all with the affection of Christ Jesus (Phil. 1:8 RSV).

> But we were *gentle* among you, like a mother caring for her little children. We *loved* you so much that we were delighted to share with you not only the gospel of God but our lives as well, because you had become so *dear* to us (1 Thess. 2:7,8).

This heart concern for people will allow nothing to prevent communication of the gospel. The building of new Christians will also be the focus of much intense effort. One of the most moving times of my life was when I was on campus one day with an experienced Christian worker. As we were walking across the campus, I noticed his silence. Looking at him more closely, I discovered tears running down his face. He shared with me his burden for those young people — a burden that brought him to tears. This is what I mean about having a real love for people. Jesus' weeping over Jerusalem is another example of this. The true, faithful disciple can never remain aloof and detached.

CHECKLIST FOR FAITHFUL MEN

_____ 1. A hunger for God's Word

_____ 2. A thirst for holy living

_____ 3. A desire for greater knowledge of God

_____ 4. A basic commitment to the lordship of Christ

_____ 5. A desire to be used by God

_____ 6. A love for people

Fig. 1

A sound analysis of these criteria should help you find the faithful men you are seeking. It should be stressed that each of these criteria will only be in seed form in the new Christian. Obviously, as a Christian grows in Christ these characteristics will become deeper and more complete. Yet I believe the seeds of such characteristics are discernible, even in a newer Christian's life. Never disciple by default! If a person does not meet the standard, don't work with him in the area of discipleship training.

A final word about choosing whom to disciple. Make sure your decision is the object of much prayer. Few decisions you make will have as far-reaching implications as this one. For multiplication to occur, you must choose faithful men. Follow the example in Luke 6:12,13:

> One of those days Jesus went out into the hills to pray, and spent the night praying to God. When morning came, he called his disciples to him and chose twelve of them, whom he also designated apostles.

LEVELS OF DISCIPLESHIP TRAINING

After having picked out those whom God calls you to disciple, what exactly are you trying to achieve? Setting up goals for your ministry of discipleship is extremely important. Discipleship training is the preparation process to produce multiplication. This process is gauged by the progress of a Christian through six distinct levels of spiritual development. (See diagram on following page.)

Level I is the achievement of effectiveness in evangelism, the product of both training and experience. This level is fundamental. Level II is achieving a degree of consistency in growth in the life of a believer. Although consistency isn't the same as perfection, it does imply an overall direction of visible growth in a Christian's life, in spite of periodic stumblings. Level III is the development of a motivator — the Christian who is beginning to motivate others for involvement. Level IV occurs when a Christian begins to conserve the fruit of evangelism through

29

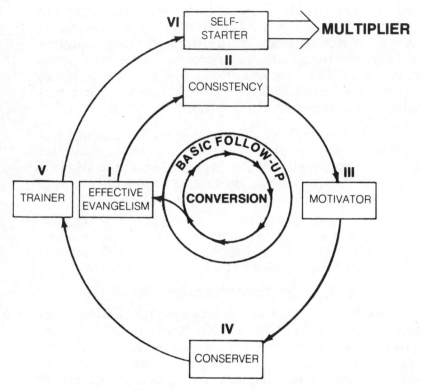

FIG. 2   LEVELS OF DISCIPLESHIP TRAINING

personal follow-up of a new Christian. Level V is reached when the person becomes a trainer — that is, he begins to transfer ministry training to others (2 Tim. 2:2). Level VI is that stage when the person you are working with becomes a self-starter — he has become truly independent of you and is being fruitful and effective totally apart from any input from you.[5]

My purpose in this book is to touch on those things necessary to bring a person through all of these levels and into a truly multiplying ministry.

Notes

[1]Some excellent material on what a true disciple is can be found in the following books:

> Kenneth Kinghorn, *Dynamic Discipleship* (Grand Rapids: Baker, 1975).

> Francis Schaeffer, *True Spirituality* (Wheaton, Ill.: Tyndale, 1971).

[2]Insights into methodology can be given in the following books:

> A. B. Bruce, *The Training of the Twelve* (Grand Rapids: Kregel, 1971).

> Robert Coleman, *The Master Plan of Evangelism* (Old Tappan, N.J.: Revell, 1963).

[3]Gary Kuhne, *The Dynamics of Personal Follow-up* (Grand Rapids: Zondervan, 1976), pp. 16–29

> See also:

> Waylon Moore, *New Testament Follow-up* (Grand Rapids: Eerdmans, 1963), pp. 61–69.

> Dawson Trotman, *Born to Reproduce* (Colorado Springs: Navigators, 1974).

[4]Kuhne, *Dynamics of Personal Follow-up*, pp. 145–206.

[5]A fuller discussion on these levels can be found in Kuhne, *Dynamics of Personal Follow-up*, pp. 132–37.

2

Life Transference

> But we were gentle among you, like a mother caring for her little children. We loved you so much that we were delighted to share with you not only the gospel of God but our lives as well, because you had become so dear to us. (1 Thess. 2:7,8).

In these verses in the first letter to the Christians at Thessalonica, Paul identifies the foundational factor in building disciples. Although there are many doctrinal truths a new Christian must learn and many ministry skills he must gain, these in themselves will not produce a disciple. A disciple can be produced only through the obedient application of the Word of God to his life. Our role as disciplers is to help a person become an obedient doer, not just hearer, of the Word of God. The key to achieving this obedient application in a growing Christian's life is to be willing to pour your life into him. This sharing of your life is called "life transference" and is so important to discipleship development that multiplication is nearly impossible without it.

THE CONCEPT OF TRANSFERENCE

What does it mean to transfer your life into the life of another? Actually, life transference involves several elements. Perhaps it could be best summarized as "the living communication of data." A Christian must work and live closely enough with the new Christian to show him in an obvious way the real-life implications of the commands of God being taught. Truly effective teaching is increasingly being recognized in secular studies to be the product of just such a combination of information and the real-life exposure to the practical applications of knowledge.

Once a new Christian has moved beyond the stage of personal follow-up and into the process of discipleship training, the major role of the discipler becomes counseling the growing Christian on how to make practical applications of the Word of God to his life. In life transference, the major purpose of your ministry is to show practical applications, and this will be a product of both example setting and issue confronting.

1. Issue Confronting

Issue confronting is that part of the discipler's work of getting to know the new Christian well enough to see where the applications of God's Word are to be made in his life. It is not enough to tell someone he must be patient. You must also tell him where he is impatient and how to become patient in such areas. Thus the issue confronting us is making practical applications of God's Word to problem areas in a growing Christian's life. This would be impossible apart from the close personal relationship developed through discipleship training.

Perhaps an example of issue confronting would be helpful. One important Christian virtue is patience. To tell Mary that she should be patient would be true, but inadequate. We must show her on the personal level what it means for her to be patient. Perhaps Mary has a problem with overreacting to the disobedience of her children. An issue-confronting approach would be to say, "Mary, God calls upon you to be a patient person. Let me show you what this means. Remember the way you blew up at your children this morning? It is in just that type of an area of your life that God is desiring you to practice patience in the power of His Spirit."

It is ministry on this practical, personal level that will do much to develop Christlikeness in people. But realize that such a ministry demands that you have built an honest, open relationship with the growing Christian and that you know enough about his life to make specific applications of God's Word to his particular situations. Much time in prayer and study is required to make such applications of truth to specific, real-life problems. The Bible describes such an activity as demonstrating wisdom, and God promises us help:

> If any of you lacks wisdom, he should ask God, who gives generously to all without finding fault, and it will be given to him (James 1:5).

2. Example Setting

Example setting is the other aspect of transferring your life to another. As a growing Christian observes your life style and conduct, he gains valuable, practical insights into what it means to live the Christian life. Example setting is a key point in effective follow-up ministry, but is even more important to disciple-building. Scripture abounds with the emphasis on example setting for development of disciples.

> Don't let anyone look down on you because you are young, but set an example for the believers in speech, in life, in love, in faith and in purity (1 Tim. 4:12).

> Remember your leaders, who spoke the word of God

> to you. Consider the outcome of their way of life and imitate their faith (Heb. 13:7).
> ... but in order to make ourselves a model for you to follow (2 Thess. 3:9).

A living demonstration of what Christianity means is far more effective than just an explanation. This principle lies behind much of Christ's discipling ministry. He called His disciples to follow Him, and as a result of their following Him, He would make them into effective servants. In fact, Christ specifically stated that one of His major reasons for calling His disciples was that they might be able to just "spend time" with Him (see Mark 3:13,14). Robert Coleman, in his excellent study of the discipling ministry of Christ, feels that such example setting, such association, was the essence of Christ's methodology.[1]

I have often heard Christians say that they don't want others to follow them, but rather they want them to follow Christ. At first glance this seems to be a humble, pious response. Yet I believe it to be inadequate. Paul felt no qualms about challenging people to follow his example, as the following verse clearly shows:

> ... but to give you in our conduct an example to imitate (2 Thess. 3:9 RSV).

The truth is that the godly example of mature believers is a reflection of the example of Christ. Actually, our growth in Christlikeness provides a type of incarnation of truth for the believer to follow. There is so much more that is "caught" rather than taught in the disciple-building process. Example setting sets up a fertile environment for catching more of the real thing, i.e. the fullness of maturity in Christ.

Such example setting not only shows an incarnation of the truth to stimulate application on the part of the disciple, but it also demonstrates the reality and possibility of change in a believer's life. When the growing Christian can observe your increasing victory and transformation in certain areas of your life, he gains invaluable edification and encouragement in the dynamics of change in his own life. This is why discipling doesn't demand that you be perfect, but does demand that you be consistently growing into true Christlikeness.

3. Total Life Change

I believe it is also important to recognize that such pouring of your life into another is a process that affects the total person. The new Christian with whom you are working is made up of many parts — social, mental, physical, emotional, spiritual, etc. — all forming together an interrelated, cohesive whole. The reality of regeneration should affect the whole person being ministered to. Thus you must be concerned with the entirety of one's life to see the totality of change that Christ promises. This demands involvement with a person even in parts of his life that don't seem to relate to the spiritual.

Let's assume you are teaching your disciple to be a good steward of his money, and also that he can trust God's provision for his future needs. While this teaching definitely affects the spiritual dimension of his life, it also affects and is affected by nonspiritual dimensions. Perhaps the disciple has never learned to budget and thus makes bad use of his income. To require a tithe and yet not aid him in learning to budget would be to court financial disaster. We must work with a person's total life to see applications of the Word made. Such practical and seemingly obvious principles are seldom followed by those with whom I have had contact in the past years.

As I study the New Testament, I find that disciple-building through life transference includes other things in addition to example setting and issue confronting. There is an obvious need for formal teaching on doctrine and training in ministry skills. Yet as the person moves through the levels of discipleship training, the need for such teaching and training ceases with the increasing stability of the growing Christian. Thus example setting and issue confronting are of longer duration in a discipling ministry.

4. Counseling Ministry

In the period of time necessary to go through the levels of discipleship training described in chapter 1, our training is achieved by several types of training relationships. At the beginning of our work with the new Christian, we follow a very structured format because his most pressing need is for information regarding his faith. We also will strive to meet in an unstructured format with the new and growing Christian to build a close friendship with him. As he continues to grow and moves into the phase of ministry I have called discipleship training, the format of our meetings increasingly becomes counseling oriented. Such a work I call counseling one-to-one ministry. It is this type of ministry that is necessary for life transference.[2]

The format of counseling one-to-one ministry is geared to stimulate character development. This means helping a person to detect areas in his life that need to be dealt with for increasing maturity. Stimulation and encouragement are also included. It takes involvement and time. You must be making personal applications of God's Word to your own life in order to be effective in helping someone else do it. There is a minimum of structure in this form of ministry.

THE CHARACTER OF THE DISCIPLER

Since the key to life transference is simply spending time with an individual and allowing demonstration to occur, the maturity of the person doing the disciple-building is extremely important. As I mentioned previously, more is caught than taught, and we must be careful to infect others with the right "disease." It is necessary that you be at a point in maturity (and going beyond it) that you wish others to arrive at. In disciple-building, like will produce like. Christ clearly had this in mind in the following verse:

> A disciple is not above his teacher, but every one when he is fully taught will be like his teacher (Luke 6:40 RSV).

Since this principle is true, the issue is clear: What must your life be like to be worth reproducing? What should you be like to be worth transferring to someone else? The key to answering these questions is to examine what the Word of God identifies as the characteristics, or qualifications, for spiritual leadership. Since the Bible clearly stresses the role of example and the unavoidable effects of it, those who are put into spiritual leadership should reflect certain characteristics to insure a positive transference. Thus, for our purposes, a study of life transference in discipleship training should obviously focus on these characteristics.

Interestingly, gifts are never mentioned in relationship to choosing leaders in the early church. Those passages dealing with qualifications for spiritual leaders such as deacons or elders never mention them. In all cases, spiritual maturity is the issue, not gifts. There are three major passages dealing with such qualifications, and the remainder of this chapter will examine them individually. The passages I will consider are Titus 1:5–9; 1 Timothy 3:1–7; and 1 Peter 5:1–3.

Titus 1:5-9:

> This is why I left you in Crete, that you might amend what was defective, and appoint elders in every town as I directed you, if any man is blameless, the husband of one wife, and his children are believers and not open to the charge of profligate or insub-

39

ordinate. For a bishop, as God's steward, must be blameless; he must not be arrogant or quick-tempered or a drunkard or violent or greedy for gain, but hospitable, a lover of goodness, master of himself, upright, holy, and self-controlled; he must hold firm to the sure word as taught, so that he may be able to give instruction in sound doctrine, and also to confute those who contradict it (RSV).

Let's examine each of these characteristics in greater depth.

1. *A Discipler Is to Be Blameless.* The word *blameless* means "to be unable to be called into account." The root idea is that a person's life is to be lived in such a way that no charge can be made against him. The implication of this word here is that the Christian should be living the type of life where no one would think of charging him with evil. Thus the impression of one's life on others is in focus. It is not enough to be able to be acquitted if charged. We should not be in a position to be charged with evil in the first place. This idea is repeated in 1 Thessalonians 5:22 "Abstain from all appearance of evil" (KJV).

Let me share a practical example of applying this particular characteristic. A student I had been discipling came to me for counseling on a problem he was facing. He had been building relationships with various non-Christian students, seeking to win them to Christ. He had been invited to two parties by these people he was witnessing to. Both parties would certainly be characterized by some drinking by non-Christians present. One party was to be large, attended by many people he didn't know. The other would be small, attended exclusively by his friends. Which party should he attend, or should he go to neither? After some discussion, we concluded that the first party was out of the question. Since so many attending wouldn't know him, they would not be watching him closely. Thus all they would remember was that he attended and assume he went along with the drinking. The second party, however, was different. There everyone knew him and would be very aware he wasn't drinking. He could continue to build relationships, yet be blameless in their eyes. He decided to go to the second. While he was at the party, he won one of his friends to Christ. This practical type of mature decision-making demonstrates the characteristic of blamelessness. We must not only do right things, but also be wise about the appearance we are making.

2. *The Discipler Is to Be Devoted.* Another characteristic discussed in this passage is the need to be the husband of one wife. For some readers the literal application of this passage is impossible to apply since you are not married or are a woman. Many expositors believe this passage is referring to being a "one woman" type of man. The point of the passage is not to teach against polygamy, as this is dealt with other places. I believe the idea being developed is that of commitment, being devoted. The focus is on the quality of the relationship, not just the singleness of it. A leader must be demonstrating to others commitment and devotion in his marriage relationship to infect others with such traits in their relationships to Christ. Nothing will kill a leader's effectiveness and credibility like a shallow marriage relationship. Yet the Christian community is filled with examples of this problem.

3. *The Discipler Is to Be Respected by His Family.* The next characteristic is the type of relationship between the leader and his children. Again we are looking at a characteristic that is not universally applicable because not all Christians are married and have children. The biblical lists of characteristics must be inclusive of all relevant qualifications so those in different circumstances may still be evaluated. The leader's children are to be believers, or a better translation, "tending toward belief." This would show fulfillment of the command and promise of

Proverbs 22:6:

> Train up a child in the way he should go, and when he is old he will not depart from it.

The idea here is not perfection in children, but their tending toward belief in Christ.

The children are also not to be profligate or insubordinate. The key idea is that of respectfulness toward the parent. If the children do not respect the parent, something is seriously wrong. The child knows the parent better than anyone else. If this knowledge causes, or at least doesn't stop disrespect, generally there is something wrong with the parent's life. It is possible that the parent failed to faithfully carry out his responsibility in the past, and thus the church should hesitate to entrust them with spiritual responsibility now. At the very least, an examination should be made to determine if the child's life style is attributable to parental failure. These are harsh, yet clear words. It is important to realize, however, that the idea here is not perfection. All children are disrespectful to their parents at times. The problem discussed here is a consistent life style of disrespect.

4. *The Discipler Is Not to Be Arrogant.* The spiritual leader is not to be characterized by arrogance. The Greek word in this case means "to be dominated by self interest." Trench, in his word studies, says this word implies that a person is arrogant and dogmatic in areas where he shouldn't be. What he has deduced to be true has to be right, with no further discussion. No wonder this is highlighted in the negative when discussing spiritual leadership! Because of example, the effects of such arrogance could be devastating to Christian growth.

I have seen many examples of this characteristic and the danger it presents to disciple-building. I remember a particular pastor who was able to speak authoritatively on many issues because of his scholarly background. Before long he began to speak with equal dogmatism on issues the Scripture gives us no right to be dogmatic about. Soon everyone was forced to agree with him down to the smallest detail, or risk being belittled and forced out of the church. The people attending that church began to reflect this arrogant dogmatism. Unfortunately, this characteristic is easily reproduced.

There is a great need to determine where to be rigid and where not to be rigid. In the gaining of such discernment we are bound to make mistakes. Such mistakes can be beneficial if we portray an attitude of humility in admitting our mistakes and changing. This will help the growing disciple to be more flexible in his life as well.

5. *The Discipler Must Handle Anger Correctly.* He must not be quick-tempered. The word means "being prone to anger." The picture here is of someone having a habit of resorting to temper quickly when things are not quite right in his circumstances. The problem is being habitually quick to utilize anger in dealing with conflicts. This problem is often seen by how fast a person gets red and explodes whenever he is disputed with. If such an individual gains a position of spiritual leadership, he will breed a whole batch of quick-exploders in the church. Thus we see the seriousness of this issue for those who are involved in disciple building.[3]

6. *The Discipler Is to Be Temperate.* Not being a drunkard is the next attribute mentioned in this passage. The idea behind the word in the Greek is temperance. God wants us to be temperate people. This passage is not talking about abstinence, only temperance, and it applies to more than the issue of alcohol. It is possible to become drunk or intoxicated, or addicted to other things. Christians can fall prey to drunkenness in the pursuit of money, watching television, eating, and a host of other areas. The disciple-builder is to demonstrate the role of temperance

in all things. A growing Christian must recognize the dangers of slavery to various activities in his life. The following verse repeats this challenge:

> "Everything is permissible for me" — but I will not be mastered [enslaved] by anything (1 Cor. 6:12b).

7. *The Discipler Is Not to Be Contentious.* Another quality of the discipler examined here is that he is not to be violent. Other translations say "not to be a striker," or they use the word *pugnacious,* but they are all referring to the same thing — that a qualification for spiritual leadership is to not be contentious. The idea is similar to the idea of not being quick-tempered, yet gives an added dimension to it. The word picture in the Greek is that the discipler is not to go around with a chip on his shoulder. Personally I find it easy to have spiritual chips on my shoulder, and I'm sure you do as well. Perhaps it's a pet doctrinal issue or some other thing that you're just waiting for someone to bring up and all of a sudden you become contentious. You quickly strike out at them, either physically or verbally, to deal with the issue. That's the idea being prohibited in this passage. The intent to do violence, not just the action of violence, is what is being warned against.

I remember a director of the youth program in a local church who demonstrated this characteristic of violence. He kept kids in line by threatening them with a punch in the nose. He often acted like he was about to do just that and those around him would hold him back. He had a youth group that behaved, but at what price? Perhaps you know similar individuals who seek to bring about conformity by threats of verbal or even physical violence. A chip on the shoulder or pugnaciousness is a terrible thing to reproduce. The Christian life has no room for bullies or fighters.

8. *The Discipler Is Not to Be Greedy.* Disciplers are warned against being greedy for gain. The particular focus

of the Greek word is financial or material gain. The idea is letting your life be dominated by a desire for financial or material success. When financial gain becomes a major goal in your life, you can't help but have this goal reproduced in others. Commitment to the lordship of Christ would certainly be difficult to produce when money becomes a god. This attitude is reflected not only by seeking financial gain in the secular world, but also by an unhealthy concern for finances in the church. It is possible to replace trust in God's ongoing provision for our needs with the tangible security of a bank account. Such a shift would be quick to be accepted and copied by the growing Christian who is having problems trusting God for financial provision in the first place. How deadening such an example could be from a leader!

9. *The Discipler Is to Be Hospitable.* Hospitality means "to be fond of offering hospitality." Do you really enjoy being hospitable to people? The idea is not just whether you are doing it, but whether you are fond of doing it. The implication here is hospitality without any thought of return or even any chance of return.

This characteristic — being fond of hospitality without any thought of return — is clearly portrayed in the book *Hidden Art* by Edith Schaeffer, Dr. Francis Schaeffer's wife.[4] In this book Mrs. Schaeffer describes how in the early years of Dr. Schaeffer's ministry, when he was still a pastor here in the United States, they lived in Grove City, Pennsylvania, along one of the rail lines. She would often see hobos walking along the tracks. She made a practice of showing hospitality to these individuals by making lunches for them. She wouldn't just give them a bowl of soup, but went beyond this to do such things as putting a flower on the tray. She went out of her way to brighten their day, all the while knowing there was no way they could return her hospitality. In fact, she might never see them again. She was just fond of showing hospitality, or going out of her way to do things for other people.

The basic principle behind hospitality is desiring to help people without any thought of return. Obviously this is a characteristic of life worth transferring, since this is an important attitude to reproduce in a new Christian. The willingness to go out of our way to do things for others is the same characteristic of the Good Samaritan as told in the parable of Christ. We are to go out of our way to be hospitable.

Another implication of hospitality is to have people over for dinner, or to provide lodging for visitors. Some commentators think that this particular word also implied in the early church a willingness to open one's home to meetings. This was needed since the early church was not often characterized by having formal buildings. The body of believers moved from home to home for the different meetings that were held. Whether this specific meaning has application today depends on whether your church has a building. The principle is to be willing to be open with the things God has blessed you with. It could be your house, your food, or your money.

10. *The Discipler Is to Love Goodness.* The spiritual leader is to be a lover of goodness. Some translations say a lover of "good" rather than a lover of "goodness." The word in the Greek has an active rather than a passive connotation; it means not only having a nice disposition, but also actively thinking on good. I think Philippians 4:8 presents this same principle of active mind set:

> Finally, brothers, whatever is true, whatever is noble, whatever is right, whatever is pure, whatever is lovely, whatever is admirable — if anything is excellent or praiseworthy — think about such things.

The mind set of an individual is of key importance in the process of disciple-building. Having the proper mind set is something you want to be reproducing in the life of that growing Christian. He needs to develop the right mind set not only in specifically spiritual things, but also good things in general. The idea is to fill our minds with honorable, edifying thoughts that result in praise of God.

11. *The Discipler Is to Have a Sober Mind.* Another characteristic important in the discipler is to be a master of himself. Some translations use the word *sober* here; others use the word *sensible.* The Greek word means "a sober mind." A person ought to have self-control in the mind. This thought certainly ties back into the mind-set idea previously discussed, but also includes the additional idea of wisdom. Many commentators propose that the meaning went beyond simple sobriety. The word meant that a person was characterized by wisdom in the use of his mind and body. The idea was the opposite of frivolousness, or of operating one's life without concern. The principle was that a person was to be wise in the living of all aspects of his life so he demonstrated Christian self-control as a total-life principle.

This is crucial in developing disciples. Christianity was not meant to be relegated to a certain compartment of your life. Regeneration affects the total person. The growing believer will tend to copy your life in all areas, not only the specifically spiritual. Have you thought through seriously what it means to be a Christian in all aspects of your life, or are you frivolous and unconcerned in the total stewardship of your time and life?

12. *The Discipler Is to Be Holy and Upright.* The next two words describing attributes of spiritual leadership are the words *upright* and *holy.* The meanings of these words are obvious. The idea is to be living a holy and upright life. The implications in life transference are also obvious.

13. *The Discipler Is to Be Self-controlled.* The next characteristic we come to is that of being self-controlled. Certainly a number of the characteristics we've looked at

already had the implications of self-control in them, yet this passage uses the word in a specific way. It is the same word that is used in Galatians 5:22,23, discussing the fruit of the Spirit:

> But the fruit of the Spirit is love, joy, peace, patience, kindness, goodness, faithfulness, gentleness and *self-control*. Against such things there is no law.

Self-control means keeping things in hand, having power over the wrong things, keeping oneself in tow. The idea of self-control present here is the idea of victory over sinful desires. Since self-control is described in the fruit of the Spirit, it is obvious where it comes from.

14. *The Discipler Is to Hold Firm the Word.* Another distinction that's worth transferring is that the discipler holds firm to the Word of God. Obviously, in order to hold it firm, we have to know it. The command here isn't to clutch our Bibles so tightly that nobody can pull them away from us. Rather, the idea is to really understand the Bible, be committed to its truth and its authority. There's no room in spiritual leadership for those who are less than committed to the authority of the Word of God. For unless disciplers are committed to the belief that the Bible is really the verbally inspired, infallible Word of God, their example will act like a cancer destroying the objective faith of the body of believers.[5]

So, this characteristic of knowing the Word of God and accepting its authority and truthfulness is one thing you definitely want to reproduce. God's Word is the rule of life. When the Bible says to do something, you do it obediently; and when it says not to do something, you don't do it. You want to develop that commitment to the authority of the Bible in the life of the disciple. For all the reasons I've already discussed about discipleship, this commitment must be there. Without it the Christian will not grow.

If you accept the Word of God as final and authoritative in all that it speaks about, if you are thus holding firm to the Word of God, then you are able to do the next two things which are also characteristics of spiritual leadership.

15. *The Discipler Is to Be a Sound Teacher.* In having a life that's worth transferring, you must be able to give instruction (or exhort) in sound doctrine. You must know doctrine and be able to communicate it. The implication for the discipler at this point is not limited to the group teaching level, being able to get up in front of a group and give a doctrinal lesson. The implication includes understanding doctrine to the point of being able to use it even on a one-on-one level, to counsel and correct a person.

To teach effectively on sound doctrine you must be able to communicate clearly and know much more than you are communicating at any point in time. This is the safety check for knowing whether or not what you are communicating is indeed sound doctrine.

16. *The Discipler Is to Confute Error.* The second of these two things is that you are able to confute those who contradict sound doctrine. The word *confute* means to convict to the point that you bring about confession. The word confute is similar to the word rebuke in 2 Timothy 3:16, where the word means to convict a person successfully about the truth. So it is necessary that you know the Word well enough to confute those who contradict it. This means knowing how to deal with the cultist, or the atheist, etc. This is what you'll want to reproduce in the life of the disciple you're working with.

An ability to use the Word of God was certainly a key discipling tool that Christ used with His disciples. He utilized the Word of God to confute the Pharisees, the scribes, and the Sadducees, showing clearly where they were departing from what God intended. It is important to understand that Christ used the Word of God to confute those in error. Error must be dealt with in such an objective manner rather than just through subjective reasoning and speculation.

You must also see that this confuting was not done in an obnoxious way. Turn to 2 Timothy 2:24:

> And the Lord's servant must not quarrel but he must be kind to everyone, able to teach, not resentful.

This verse emphasizes a gentle and directive confrontation, in which your communication is such that the truth is clear and their rejection will also be clear. But if you approach those in error in an obnoxious way, their defences will be up, and they will not understand what you're saying. They are never going to repent and come to the point of truth if this happens, because they have never understood the truth. The idea is to have a gentle confrontation that is corrective enough to make the point clear. You must be directive, but you don't want to be obnoxious.

Your goal should be the same as Paul's, as seen in 2 Corinthians 10:5:

> We destroy arguments and every proud obstacle to the knowledge of God, and take every thought captive to obey Christ (RSV).

You want to destroy every proud obstacle and get rid of everything that prevents a person from clearly understanding that he has no grounds on which to stand for continued rebellion against God. The idea here is being able to confute those who try to contradict sound doctrine based on the truths of the Word of God, in such a way that they will understand where they are wrong. By this understanding, God may perhaps grant them the opportunity to come to know the truth. Some might continue in rebellion against God and His Word, but at least they will clearly understand that they are in rebellion against it. This is confuting that brings the person to the point of repentance.

There's no way you can do this until you know the Word of
God and are able to teach it. Only then can you apply it to
specific problems.

This characteristic of spiritual leadership is difficult
to achieve. It will be in just such areas of conflict that you
will feel most intensely your lack of knowledge. Yet you
must not resort to dealing with conflict any other way. The
growing disciple must see the importance of knowing the
Word. Although it is difficult to do, it is something you can
be consistently working toward, and it will be a by-
product of your continued growth and knowledge of the
Word.

1 Timothy 3:2-7:

A number of characteristics are repeated in this passage
that were examined in Titus 1:5–9. I will focus on the new
ones added in this passage.

> Now a bishop must be above reproach, the husband of
> one wife, temperate, sensible, dignified, hospitable,
> an apt teacher, no drunkard, not violent but gentle,
> not quarrelsome, and no lover of money. He must
> manage his own household well, keeping his chil-
> dren submissive and respectful in every way; for if a
> man does not know how to manage his own house-
> hold, how can he care for God's church? He must not
> be a recent convert, or he may be puffed up with
> conceit and fall into the condemnation of the devil;
> moreover he must be well thought of by outsiders,
> or he may fall into reproach and the snare of the devil
> (RSV).

17. *The Discipler Is to Be Calm.* The first new characteristic of spiritual leadership that we see is that the person
is to be temperate. The idea of the Greek word describes
someone who is calm and dispassionate. The implication
is that this person habitually uses wise caution. This caution gives rise to calmness and temperance. A similar idea
would be the biblical command to be slow to anger. This

caution brings with it such things as being slow to speak, being slow to act, and making sure you think before you talk. It is important to think before you move rather than think after you've moved, regretting what you did.

Temperate in this case is not the same thing as temperance. Temperance means not overdoing something, such as drinking, eating, etc. Temperate is the idea of calmness and wise actions. This is a good attitude to impart to a new disciple. In my life I've consistently found a problem of stepping out and saying something or trying to do something before I've really thought about it.

What a gift to someone else to demonstrate and help him develop this wise caution, building in him a calmness, a dispassionate approach to living. This does not mean a dull approach, but rather one in which they wisely use their time, their words, and other similar things.

18. *The Discipler Is to Be Gentle.* Another quality of spiritual leadership presented in this passage is the importance of being gentle, not violent. The meaning of the word *gentle* is to be forbearing, equitable, or fair. Gentle means to be considerate. One way to be gentle is to look reasonably at the facts of a situation and not act based on emotion alone. A person who is violent is usually not looking at all the facts; he's just made a snap judgment and acted on it. A spiritual leader should not make snap judgments of things. The idea is tied in somewhat with the idea of temperate. The purpose is to make a person slow to judge and wise, not as apt to fly off the handle.

19. *The Discipler Is to Be a Manager.* The next characteristic of the discipler is that he is able to manage his household. The word *manage* comes from a Greek word meaning effective superintendence. In essence, the idea is that a person had proven to be an effective supervisor of his household. His home and family are orderly, not chaotic or marked by confusion. It implies also that the children are

reasonably submissive, respectful, and obedient.

In essence, the issue here is reproducing through effective supervision in the home the type of atmosphere that God would produce there. And the way we know that the type of atmosphere God would produce in the home is the atmosphere that He wants to produce in the church. This is described for us in 1 Corinthians 14:40 when God says, "[Let] all things be done . . . in order." God is not a God of confusion but a God of peace. In other words, God's purposes are reflected in an orderly, well-organized, non-chaotic situation. The discipler should exercise great care not to develop a chaotic approach to his life. For the head of the family, family order is the criterion of judgment. To those who are not heads of families, the principle of not being chaotic or disorganized themselves is going to be the criterion. Being well organized is certainly something you want to be produced in the life of the person you're working with.

20. *The Discipler Cannot Be a New Convert.* Why shouldn't the discipler be a new convert? Because he may become puffed up with conceit and fall into the condemnation of the devil. All of us are prone to conceit no matter how mature we are. But a new Christian is more apt to have a problem with pride because he will not be able to diagnose it for what it is. This is because his discernment is minimal. In Hebrews 5:14 the mature person is described as one who through practice has been trained to make such decisions more easily and quickly. Thus, even though we are all prone to pride, the mature are able to recognize it more quickly, before it becomes a major problem.

What often happens in the church is that everyone becomes impressed by a new Christian's testimony. They think, "Well, anyone who has had that kind of a conversion experience would not fail the Lord. Let's give him this position of responsibility." Then the same old story is repeated of the brand-new Christian being given a Sunday school class to teach, or some other kind of position. They begin thinking they know something when they know little. They become set for a fall.

The term *puffed up* comes from an interesting source in the Greek. It initially described what happened when a person tried to make a fire and the smoke came up and got in his eyes, and he went away with his eyes watering. He wasn't totally blind. He could still see objects, but he couldn't see them as they really were. Everything was vague and blurry. That is the root meaning of being puffed up. This is a good word picture because it shows what pride does. Pride doesn't blind you totally, but it blinds you to the extent that you don't see things the way they really are. And whenever you don't see things the way they really are, you are in a position to be easily deceived by Satan.

A new convert cannot be in a position of leadership. I previously explained that there are various levels of discipleship training, and a growing Christian is not going to be able to reproduce himself until he attains a certain level of maturity in his own life. Reproducing is more than following certain methods; it is more than merely imparting information; it is imparting one life to another. It will not be profitable for a person to do this until he becomes mature in his own life.

How long does a person have to be a Christian before he can be a leader? It is impossible to set a definite time limit because someone can be a Christian forty years and still not be ready. A Christian who is still disobedient, still puffed up with pride, still not consistently growing, is not ready. Someone else could have been a Christian for only nine months to a year and actually be in a place where he is now able to begin to reproduce in other people. He has not attained full maturity, obviously, but he has grown sufficiently to the point where he is able to reproduce in other people. It is hard to say definitely when a person reaches a point where he is able to reproduce, but I suppose that after a year of knowing the Lord, one ought to be in a position to begin to reproduce in other people. He is not yet totally independent, perhaps, but still in a position where he can begin to assume some spiritual leadership.

21. *The Discipler Is to Have a Good Public Image.* The next requirement of a spiritual leader is to be well thought of by outsiders. Isn't it odd that one of the criteria for spiritual leadership, for having a life worth transferring, has something to do with people outside the body of believers? When I first read this passage, I didn't understand this point. I began to ask myself what the Bible taught me about the world. The Bible certainly said the world would hate and persecute us, just as it did Christ. How could these be reconciled?

After considerable thinking about this paradox, I began to understand the implications. If a Christian is not well thought of by outsiders, there is something seriously wrong. Although the world might hate us, it should never morally distrust us. The principle here implies we are to be held above reproach by all. In other words, even at the time Christ was crucified, Pilate had to say, "I find no fault with this man. There's nothing wrong with Him." His crucifixion was not brought about by the Romans because they had questions about His sincerity or morality. It was brought about by those religious leaders who were convicted deeply by the truth He was communicating, and they wanted to get rid of the truth, to blot it out. So the implication here is that if the world doesn't trust someone, we had better not trust him either, regardless of how mature he seems to be. There is something wrong if the world doesn't trust him; there are generally good reasons why. If a person isn't well thought of by outsiders, we'd better take care.

We ought to be living lives that breed trust in other people, rather than mistrust. As Christians we should be careful not to act so that the world wonders what's happening. It's the idea of trust that's important. Is your manner of life such that people outside trust you?

1 Peter 5:1-4:

> So I exhort the elders among you, as a fellow elder and a witness of the sufferings of Christ as well as a partaker in the glory that is to be revealed. Tend the flock of God that is your charge, not by constraint but willingly, not for shameful gain but eagerly, not as domineering over those in your charge but being examples to the flock (RSV).

22. *The Discipler Must Desire to Serve God.* Do you really have an enthusiasm from the heart in being obedient to the will of the Father? The principle in focus is your attitude toward service. Are you willing to be obedient, or aren't you? Are you serving God because your arm is being twisted or because of the love of God in your heart? This attitude of willingness must be present if you want to guard against developing a legalistic attitude in the life of the person you're trying to disciple. An effective safeguard against legalism is to stress right motivation. And motivation is best communicated through example.

23. *The Discipler Must Not Be Motivated by Pride.* The characteristic of not leading for the sake of shameful gain focuses on gain in the sense of ego. The gain is in esteem, being elevated to a position of respect and awe. Do the Christians around you view you with awe because you're so sharp and in this position of leadership? Do you enjoy it when they verbalize what a tremendous Christian you are? Why do you do what you do? If it's for pride-building purposes, then it's wrong. Be careful that this is not your motivation. I must admit that I am convinced we can never totally overcome the taint of pride in this life. When it becomes a *major* motivation, there are real problems.

24. *The Discipler Must Not Be Domineering.* The idea

of domineering is best seen as lording it over others. This is not a prohibition against being an authority figure, since this is clearly your role. Rather, the focus is on mannerisms. It is ridiculous to claim to be a spiritual leader but not be authoritative. In order to be a leader, you have to be authoritative. God is concerned about the way you use the authority. You are to be a leader, but not a domineering person. A shepherd leads the flock, he doesn't push it.

So the focus here is to make sure that you are leading, not pushing. Lording it over others only results in perpetual dependence on you by the younger Christian. If you will remember some of the other teachings on discipleship, one thing you are striving for is independence in the growing Christian's life, getting him to the point where he is independent of you and dependent on God. You can prevent this goal from occurring by your mannerism of leading. If you are lording it over the young Christian, you will merely reinforce his tendency to be dependent on you.

25. *The Discipler Must Be an Example.* This final emphasis — on being an example to the flock — sums up all the other principles, puts them all together. Each of these various characteristics was meant to be modeled and reproduced. In reality, life transference takes place by example. If you read through Paul's Epistles, you will find Paul consistently pushing the idea of being an example. I believe this is the way you will transfer your life. All of the other guidelines are given to make sure that your example is what you want it to be, so that you reproduce what you want to reproduce.

Of course, there are many other things that pertain to spiritual authority which are not specifically identified in these lists of characteristics. But clearly each of these characteristics applies very directly to the idea of spiritual leadership and being effective in disciple-building. How do you have a life worth transferring? By consistently and obediently developing these characteristics in your life.

The Bible is so practical. It doesn't just tell you to live a good life, but it goes beyond to tell you what specifically is meant by that. As you study the Word more, you will see that the Bible is even more specific on how to achieve these characteristics. Catching a glimpse of your responsibility to be mature in these ways is indeed sobering. In light of this perhaps a prayer is the best way to end such a discussion.

> "Lord, it is sobering to look at these things, and we do know and feel deeply the responsibility to reproduce ourselves — the responsibility of life producing life. Lord, help us to trust You, to be obedient to You, to keep motivated in our own lives, and to grow in these areas, so that we might be effective in life transference. Lord, may we be effective in our task of multiplication, and most of all, may the people we work with be truly motivated to grow in You. Lord, we desire that You receive the honor and glory. We ask this in Jesus' name. Amen."

Notes

[1]Coleman, *Master Plan of Evangelism*, pp. 38–49.

[2]For a fuller discussion of these types of relationships in personal ministry, see Kuhne, *Dynamics of Personal Follow-up*, pp. 139–41.

[3]For an excellent discussion on dealing with anger, see Jay Adams, *The Christian Counselor's Manual* (Nutley, N.J.: Presbyterian and Reformed Publishing Co., 1973), pp. 348–67.

[4]Edith Schaeffer, *Hidden Art* (Wheaton, Ill.: Tyndale House, 1975).

[5]Two excellent studies of this point can be found in the following:

> Harold Lindsell, *The Battle for the Bible* (Grand Rapids: Zondervan, 1976).
>
> Francis Schaeffer, *No Final Conflict* (Downers Grove, Ill.: InterVarsity Press, 1975).

3

Developing a
Disciplined Disciple

Have nothing to do with godless myths and old
wives' tales; rather, train yourself to be godly. For
physical training is of some value, but godliness has
value for all things, holding promise for both the
present life and the life to come (1 Tim. 4:7,8).

If there is a single theme on Christian growth that characterizes the Word of God, it is the emphasis on disciplined
obedience to the commands of God. From the wilderness
wanderings, through the time of the Psalms and Proverbs,
through the Prophets, through the earthly ministry of
Christ, to the teachings of Paul in the Epistles, the clear
stress is on consistent obedience to the truth. A disci
plined practice of holy living is what God intends for the
Christian desiring to be a true disciple.

In spite of the clear emphasis of Scripture on the role
of discipline in achieving a godly life, the present genera-
tion of Christians seem to be in a constant search for a
shortcut. Many believe that there is some type of crisis

experience to be sought that will produce without effort the godliness and maturity desired. Perhaps this results from our society's preoccupation with finding the easier, quicker way to do everything. Although this attitude is not wrong in certain other areas, the revelation of God regarding growth cannot be improved upon or speeded up.

DISCIPLINE AND CHRISTIAN LIVING

First Timothy 4:7 gives the key for solving this problem. In a clear statement on growth, Paul tells Timothy to "train" himself in godliness. The root meaning of the word *train* is to exercise consistently, to be involved in disciplined practice. Thus it is clear that Paul, under inspiration of the Holy Spirit, identified the consistent, disciplined practice of godliness as the means of achieving true maturity.

I am not trying to minimize the role of the Holy Spirit in Christian growth through this emphasis on disciplined obedience. Only as the Holy Spirit empowers us can we be truly effective in keeping God's commandments. What I am trying to point out is the fact that we as Christians are commanded to play an active, cooperative role in our growth with Christ. God never implies we are to have a passive role in our maturity. Perhaps Hebrews 5:14 shows this more clearly than any other passage.

> But solid food is for the *mature*, for those who have their faculties *trained by practice* to distinguish good from evil (RSV).

In his Epistles Paul gives three major illustrations of the role of disciplined living in Christian growth: the examples of a soldier, an athlete, and a farmer. It is well worth the time to examine these three examples in more depth. We find them identified in 2 Timothy 2:3–6:

> Share in suffering as a good soldier of Christ Jesus. No soldier on service gets entangled in civilian pursuits,

since his aim is to satisfy the one who enlisted him. An athlete is not crowned unless he competes according to the rules. It is the hard-working farmer who ought to have the first share of the crops (RSV).

The soldier was on active duty, not on furlough or in the reserves. Warfare was his constant occupation. There was never a time when he was not on the alert. The phrase *on service* literally means "living in temporary quarters." Any type of involvement that hindered his ability to go immediately wherever his commander directed was to be forsaken. The application of this example to the Christian life is obvious. We are also on active duty all the time (see Ephesians 6): we must constantly be struggling against the enemy. We also are in temporary quarters: our citizenship is in heaven (Phil. 3:20), and we are no longer of this world. As Christians we must be careful not to become entangled in those activities which hinder our effectiveness in serving our King.

The athlete lived a strenuous and demanding life. He practiced every day for years to prepare for the race. In ancient Greece the athletes lived separated lives away from the world for ten months before the games. There were set training rules and an athlete was disqualified from competition if he broke them. All this work was motivated by a desire for acclaim by his fellow-man.

This example of the athlete gives us important insights for the Christian life. It is a strenuous and demanding life. In fact, it is a supernatural kind of life. Only as we are drawing on the power which the Holy Spirit imparts to us do we find it possible to live effective Christian lives. There is no room for laziness in this life. We are also to live separated lives. This separation does not mean retreating from the world around us, but rather maintaining a distinctiveness from it. As Romans 12:2 clearly commands, we must not allow ourselves to be conformed to the world. Christians have definite training rules also. We cannot choose our own method of growth. The Bible lays out the means of growth clearly, and there are no shortcuts in this process. Discipline and submissive obedience to the will of the Father is the key. Our motivation is the promise of God.

The farmer's life is characterized by hard and often wearisome toil. A farmer must learn to wait for the harvest, to keep his eyes on the future reward. So many of the necessary jobs he did had no immediate, tangible results. Yet he needed to do the work anyway if there was ever to be a harvest. The farmer operated on the *promise* of fruit. Often as Christians we will work and not see any immediate results. We must learn not to be discouraged by this. Perhaps we will sow and others will reap the fruit. The important thing is to do *what* God desires *when* He desires it. God will give fruit according to His timing. God is more interested in our faithfulness than our fruitfulness.

> Let us not become weary in doing good, for at the proper time we will reap a harvest if we do not give up (Gal. 6:9).

Examine the following verses and notice the emphasis on disciplined obedience for the maturing disciple that permeates the Bible:

> Then he said to them all: "If anyone would come after me, he must *deny* himself and *take up* his cross *daily* and *follow* me (Luke 9:23).

> Therefore, I do not run like a man running aimlessly; I do not *fight* like a man shadow boxing. No, I *beat* my body and *make it my slave* (1 Cor. 9:26,27).

> Be *watchful, stand firm* in your faith, be *courageous*, be *strong* (1 Cor. 6:13 RSV).

> *Working together* with him . . . (2 Cor. 6:1 RSV).

> *Forgetting* what is behind and *straining* toward what is ahead, I *press* on toward the goal to win the prize for which God has called me heavenward in Christ Jesus (Phil. 3:13,14).

> Remembering . . . your *work of faith* and *labor of love* and *steadfastness* of hope . . . (1 Thess. 1:3 RSV).

> . . . let us run with perseverance the race marked out for us (Heb. 12:1).

> But be *doers* of the word, and not hearers only (James 1:22 RSV).

It is imperative that your disciples become disciplined in their obedience.

Disciplined obedience is of prime importance in victorious Christian living. The Word of God places great stress on this expression of our commitment to Christ. You must help the growing disciple develop a life style of obedient living. This will not happen overnight, yet you can begin the process by making the need and method of obedience practical and clear.

WHAT DISCIPLINE REALLY IS

It is necessary to be clear in your definitions when trying to communicate the importance of discipline to a growing Christian. Webster defines obedience as the "state or act of being in submission to the will of another." This definition has some practical implications for us as Christians. First, it implies that in order to be obedient, there must be some external authority to be the object of our obedience. Second, this definition implies that true obedience is not only an outward act, but also an inner attitude of submission. This means that true obedience is the product of an inner determination to be submissive, that is, not being submissive against our will.

This issue of an external authority for our obedience

65

needs some explanation. There are two dangers growing Christians often face in this area of the source of authority for obedience. First, many Christians look within themselves for their source of authority. The main issue seems to be, "Do I feel led to obey?" Although there is truth in the fact that the Holy Spirit does guide our direction from within, we must realize this guidance will never be contrary to God's Word. Also it is not meant to be our motivation for obedience. We are to obey what God commands regardless of our inner feelings. Our external object of obedience is to be God's Word.

Second, many growing Christians make other men their external object of obedience. Although we are called to a degree of submission to our spiritual leaders, substituting them for God's Word as our external object of obedience is dangerous. Often their commands are inconsistent and contradictory, leaving a growing Christian frustrated in his obedience. Only the Bible is a totally sufficient source for our understanding of where to be obedient.

True obedience in the spiritual realm is the act of following God's will for our lives in all respects out of desire from the heart. But true obedience to God can be defined also in terms of what it does not mean:

1. True obedience is not serving God on our own terms. Often this is the way we seek to serve God, yet the growing Christian must realize that God decides on the requirements for true discipleship.

2. True obedience to God will not be a product of, nor result in, asceticism. By this I mean that we don't need to abase ourselves to be obedient to God. Obedience doesn't necessarily imply giving up fun or possessions.

3. True obedience to God is not simply outward conformity to His commandments. An important part of true obedience is that it comes from the heart. If there is not a heartfelt desire to become obedient, our outward follow-

ing of God's commandments becomes nothing more than legalism.

WHY WE SHOULD BE OBEDIENT

It is also important to answer the "why" of disciplined obedience to properly motivate the growing Christian to become obedient in his everyday life. There are three basic reasons for obedience, and they should be enough to motivate any growing Christian.

First, we should be obedient because of the fact that God loves us and is worthy of our love and obedience in return. It doesn't take much meditation on what God has done for us to be overwhelmed by His unconditional love. This should be a real factor in motivating obedience. It isn't hard to obey someone who really loves us. Examine the following verse:

> You are worthy, our Lord and God,
> to receive glory and honor and power . . . (Rev. 4:11).

Second, we should be obedient because it is a practical way to prove our love for God. This moves our love from mere lip service to actual demonstration. It is important that this proof of our love for God be present in our life. The following verses make this clear:

> This is love for God: to obey his commands. And his commands are not burdensome (1 John 5:3).

> Whoever has my commands and obeys them, he is the one who loves me. He who loves me will be loved by my Father, and I too will love him and show myself to him. (John 14:21).

Third, we should be obedient because God clearly commands us to be. This should be motivation enough for any true Christian. When God commands something, we have no option but to follow it. These verses make God's will clear in this matter:

> And now, Israel, what does the LORD your God require of you, but to fear the LORD your God, to walk in all his ways, to love him, to serve the LORD your God with all your heart and with all your soul, and to keep the commandments and statutes of the LORD, which I command you this day for your good? (Deut. 10:12,13).

> I charge you to keep this commandment without spot or blame until the appearing of our Lord Jesus Christ (1 Tim. 6:14).

> But be doers of the Word, and not hearers only, deceiving yourselves (James 1:22 RSV).

STEPS TO BECOMING AN OBEDIENT DISCIPLE

As important as it is to tell the growing Christian why he should be obedient, he must also know how to become obedient. Thus, he must be given practical suggestions on developing an obedient life. The following are basic how-to's in developing and achieving an obedient life.

Step 1: Know God's Commands

It will be extremely difficult to be obedient if a person doesn't know what to be obedient in. A growing knowledge of God's Word is necessary to see clearly what God desires for us to do. God has shown us many things about His will through His Word, as the following verses show:

> I have laid up thy word in my heart, that I might not sin against thee (Ps. 119:11).

> All Scripture is God-breathed and is useful for teaching, rebuking, correcting and training in righteousness, so that the man of God may be thoroughly equipped for every good work (2 Tim. 3:16,17).

Step 2: Look to God for Power

We cannot become truly obedient to God in all things

in our own strength. The Christian life is supernatural and is impossible to live on our own. God's power, through the enabling offered us through the indwelling Holy Spirit, is a must for effective Christian living. When we step out in faith to obey God's commands, He honors our obedience by empowering us to carry out these commands. There is a cooperative adventure in growing in Christ in which there is no room for passivity.

Step 3: Develop the Right Attitudes

Our attitudes toward obeying God and following His will can either help or hinder us in developing an obedient life. To have the right mind set is a key step in becoming obedient. The Scriptures identify several attitudes important to obedient Christian living.

1. *We should delight to do God's will.* Do you really have this attitude within? God can develop it within you if you allow Him to. The following verse is an example of this attitude:

> I delight to do thy will, O my God;
> thy law is within my heart (Ps. 40:8).

2. *We should do God's will carefully.* I find it easy to be unthinking when it comes to obedience, but it is important to be careful in our striving to do God's will. Are you careful in your implementing of God's will? There is no room for carelessness.

> This day the LORD your God commands you to do these statutes and ordinances; you shall therefore be careful to do them with all your heart and with all your soul (Deut. 26:16).

3. *We should be sincere in our obedience.* God doesn't want lip service only, but rather He desires our sincere obedience. Strive to be honest and sincere in your obedience to God's will.

> But the seed on good soil stands for those with a noble and good heart, who hear the word, retain it, and by persevering produce a crop (Luke 8:15).

IMPORTANT AREAS
FOR DISCIPLINED OBEDIENCE

There are several areas requiring disciplined obedience if the person you are working with is to become a truly effective disciple. Let's examine a few of these areas.

1. A Consistent Devotional Life

First it is imperative that the growing Christian develop a consistent devotional life. A daily time alone with God is a basic step in developing a close walk with God. It is in this time of intimate communion with God that we learn the most about Him, His will for our lives, His guidance, and His nature. Men of God agree that this daily time of devotions is the most important part of their day. The Word of God mentions in several places the need for a time alone with God and His Word.

> I rise before dawn and cry for help; I hope in thy words. My eyes are awake before the watches of the night, that I may meditate upon thy promise (Ps. 119:147,148).

> But his delight is in the law of the LORD, and on his law he meditates day and night (Ps. 1:2).

> Like newborn babes, long for the pure milk of the Word that by it you may grow in respect to salvation (1 Peter 2:2 NASB).

Much excellent material has been produced in recent years on how to have devotions, as well as a number of study aids for this need.[1]

2. Consistent Prayer Life

A second area for disciplined obedience is prayer.

This is because prayer is a basic ingredient in abundant Christian living. It will be impossible for a Christian to grow much in his relationship with Christ if this important element is not being developed.

Prayer is verbal communication with God — just talking with Him. God has established prayer to enable us to respond to Him and communicate with Him. It is, in a sense, the second part of the divine communication process. The first part is God speaking to us through His Word and His Spirit. The second part is our responding back to Him in prayer.

I have often found that prayer is misunderstood by the new Christian. He usually thinks of it as something that is dependent upon the right liturgy, terminology, or ritual. It is important to show him that prayer is simply a matter of talking with God. We don't need to know any complicated terminology or ritual. God desires for us to simply talk to Him. We must also point out that prayer is not simply a matter of saying words. Our words must be an expression of our heart. We must not only talk to God, but we must also mean what we say, otherwise prayer becomes merely an empty, meaningless procedure.

3. Consistent Involvement in Fellowship

A third aspect of disciplined obedience is getting together for Christian fellowship. No one is meant to be a loner in the Christian faith. If there is not some service going on or teaching to be received, young Christians often feel little need for merely getting together, yet this is a serious error in their thinking. It is often in the informal times of fellowship with other Christians that the most open sharing and mutual ministry takes place. (Chapter 7 will expand on the role of fellowship in the believer's life.)

4. Consistent Outreach

Evangelism is another area that requires disciplined

71

involvement. A disciple is meant to be a sharer, a communicator of the Good News. This dimension of Christian living is a difficult one in which to achieve consistency. Training and example play large roles in motivating the person you are discipling to be obedient in this area.[2]

In addition to devotions, prayer, fellowship, and outreach, the following is a list of other areas requiring disciplined involvement on the part of a growing disciple.

- Scripture memory
- Reading quality books and magazines
- Church involvement
- Stewardship
- Hospitality
- Submission to leaders

The key to helping your growing disciple become obedient in these areas is to set the example and encourage his active participation. As was stated in chapter 2, more is caught than taught, and I have found my example of obedience in these areas to be the primary motive for the new Christian to begin to do them. Positive reinforcement is also effective to stimulate his disciplined involvement. For example, praising him on his progress in memorizing Scripture will tend to stimulate further memorization. Remember that there are no substitutes for your involvement, encouragement, and example.

DEALING WITH THE UNDISCIPLINED

This chapter would be incomplete without dealing with the question of those who seem unable to become disciplined in any area, including their spiritual lives. Can these persons be helped? I often find myself dealing with such individuals, and it can be frustrating to minister and counsel with them. The remainder of this chapter will deal with this problem. It is a most perplexing one when dealing with Christians.

The problem of dealing with people who claim to

have a personality trait of being undisciplined was one of the most frustrating problems I faced in my counseling ministry. This personality trait was used as an excuse for a wide range of both spiritual and emotional problems. Generally the people who claimed to suffer from this trait seemed to feel they weren't responsible for the problems arising from it because they had no control over this personality characteristic. My attempts to help such people usually resulted in little change in their lives.

This failure to see change greatly troubled me. I am a firm believer in the total sufficiency of Scripture to meet all counseling problems (see 2 Tim. 3:16,17). I am also convinced that we are all personally responsible when we sin. We are not helpless victims of our environment or personality when it comes to temptations to sin (see 1 Cor. 10:13). Yet I must admit that this problem tried my theology. Being unwilling to make exceptions to the absolutes of Scripture, I undertook an extensive study to see if an answer to this problem could be found.

Initially I saw two possible causes for the problem of being undisciplined. First, perhaps the person doesn't realize the need to live a disciplined life. I found, however, that most were already aware of this need. I would counsel them to recognize that God wants them to be more disciplined and to go out and to it. Inevitably they came back a week later and reported, "It didn't work." This certainly wasn't the answer to the problem.

The second cause that came to my mind was that the underlying problem was disorganization. If this was the case, some training in time management and establishing priorities would solve the problem. Some reported a slight improvement, but most found little help.

I refused to give up. The Bible surely must speak to such a widespread problem. As I continued my study, I found a surprising fact: Although the Bible speaks directly to the need for discipline, it never deals directly with the problem of being undisciplined.

After further reflection, I took another track in my study. I discovered that certain problems appeared repeatedly in the lives of those I counseled who were undisciplined. Many seemed to be vaguely fearful much of the time and addicted to excuse-making. Often they were characterized by a tremendous and unwarranted pride in their knowledge of biblical truth. Some seemed to have a problem with excessive sleep. Most were chronic underachievers, never seeming to reach the goals they set. I decided to study each of these problems to see if they would shed any light on the lack of discipline.

As I studied I began to find that, although there were often several root causes identified for each problem, there was one identified which was common to all: laziness.

Were undisciplined people really lazy people? It seemed clear from the Scriptures that this was the case. Although a lack of discipline is difficult to identify as sin, laziness presents no such difficulty. *Laziness*, and related words such as *slothfulness* and *sluggard*, are clearly identified as sin in the Bible. Since laziness is sin, there is hope for solution. As I began to look at undisciplined people as being lazy and thus sinning, I found the success that eluded me in the past. When the undisciplined person could no longer placate his conscience by pretending he wasn't sinning, the way was paved to lasting solutions.

Before turning to the means of solving the problem of laziness, let's examine some verses identifying laziness as the root cause of the problems surrounding undisciplined people.

The Sin of Laziness As Found in Scripture

1. *Sleep Problems*

> Slothfulness casts into a deep sleep . . . (Prov. 19:15).

As a door turns on its hinges, so does a sluggard on his bed (Prov. 26:14).

There appears a clear relationship between excessive sleep and laziness. Of course, excessive sleep could have a medical cause and this should be checked out by a physician. Yet it is clear that an undisciplined (lazy) person will often have the accompanying problems of excessive sleep. Sleep is the lazy way to deal with stress and problems; the bed is a relatively safe place to be. There are no demands on you when you sleep. I have found that many of those who claimed to be undisciplined were nearly always tired. (See also Prov. 6:9–11.)

2. *Housework Problems*

Through sloth the roof sinks in, and through indolence the house leaks (Eccl. 10:18).

I nearly always find that getting behind in the housework is a characteristic problem of women who claim to be undisciplined. The Bible clearly shows the reason to be laziness. A household does not function well when a lazy person is around. This problem presents a graphic display of the underlying sin of laziness.

3. *Unreconciled Conditions*

Like vinegar to the teeth, and smoke to the eyes, so is the sluggard to those who send him (Prov. 10:26).

Interpersonal problems seem to dog the steps of the undisciplined individual. Inevitably a lazy person causes unreconciled conditions. I believe there are three reasons for this. First, a lazy person usually will not work at developing quality relationships with others. Second, he also resists working to change offensive personal characteristics that bar meaningful relationships from developing. Third, as this verse points out, a betrayal of trust and irresponsibility usually characterize a lazy individual. These certainly create interpersonal problems.

4. Lying

> The sluggard says, "There is a lion outside! I shall be slain in the streets!" (Prov. 22:13).

A lazy person is constantly coming up with lies to excuse his sinful behavior. The excuses are generally marked by an exaggeration of the real problems confronting him. When it comes to dealing with problems, lying is a lazy way to deal with stressful situations. Over the long run, however, lying only creates greater problems.

5. *Excessive, Groundless Fears*

> The sluggard says, "There is a lion in the road! There is a lion in the streets!" (Prov. 26:13).

This problem is closely tied in with lying. Not only is there an exaggeration of the problem facing a person, but also there is a deep fear present. I have found undisciplined individuals often characterized by excessive, groundless fears. I think these fears arise because the lazy person knows ahead of time, through past performance, that when problems arise, he will not be disciplined enough to solve them. A life pattern of failure develops, causing even small problems to become a source of fear and eventual failure. Normally in counseling the *focus* of fear is sought and dealt with. For the lazy person it's the *source*, not the focus, that is important. His basic fear could have many focuses.

6. *Arrogant Pride*

> The sluggard is wiser in his own eyes than seven men who can answer discreetly (Prov. 26:16).

A lazy, undisciplined individual is characterized by pride and an unfounded dogmatism in his own knowledge. He usually knows a little and believes he knows it all. This attitude arises because the lazy person is not disciplined enough to do the study necessary to grasp the whole picture. A dogmatism develops in politics, religion, and a host of other areas.

7. Never Achieving Goals

> The desire of the sluggard kills him for his hands refuse to labor (Prov. 21:25).

> A slothful man will not catch his prey, but the diligent man will get precious wealth (Prov. 12:27).

The lazy man will generally not achieve his goals. He sees what he wants and greatly desires it, and yet he won't do what is necessary to achieve his goals. This results in genuine despair. Here we see two important truths about the lazy man. First, he will appear to be sincere in desiring certain things; for example, he might really want to be a mature Christian. Second, even though he greatly desires something, he will not do what is necessary to accomplish it.

All the above problems usually accompanied people who came to me for counseling, claiming that their problem was that they were basically undisciplined. The Bible makes it clear that the real problem is laziness, and since laziness is sin, it can be solved.

Steps Toward Solution

Step 1: Admit Sin (1 John 1:9). The first step toward solving the problem of laziness is to admit that laziness is the problem and confess it as sin to God. The sin of laziness must not be camouflaged by calling it "being undisciplined." Until something is recognized as sin, there will be little motivation to deal with it.

Step 2: Establish Priorities and Manage Time (Eph. 5:16). The second step is to establish priorities and learn time management. Although the problem is not just that of being disorganized, disorganization is an outgrowth of laziness. Priorities and time management are the keys to solving disorganization. Chapter 5 explores this need in more detail. Proverbs 6:6–8 discusses the ant and contrasts her ways with the ways of the lazy man. Without constant exhortation, the ant knows what to do (priorities) and when to do it (time management).

Step 3: Refocus. The next step is working to refocus attention from end results to the means of achieving the results. Proverbs 21:25 clearly showed that a lazy man has goals. The problem is that he won't do what is necessary to achieve the goals. The lazy person must work to focus on the things he must be doing to end up where he desires to be. Otherwise the goals will result only in despair.

Step 4: Obedience Regardless of Feelings. The fourth step is to obey God's Word regardless of our feelings. It is important to recognize that God never gave anyone an excuse to be disobedient. Lazy people often protest, "I just didn't feel like being obedient," or, "I didn't feel like doing this." They probably didn't, yet they sinned when they weren't obedient. We need to obey God regardless of how we feel. The lazy man *can* do all things through Christ who strengthens him. Proverbs 6:6–8 shows one of the reasons the ants were used as an example — they did what was necessary without exhortation. They didn't need others constantly trying to motivate and exhort them, because they knew what had to be done and they did it. The lazy person must see the need for disciplined obedience without constant need for exhortation.

Step 5: Disciplined Living. Turn to Proverbs 13:4: "The soul of the sluggard craves, and gets nothing, while the soul of the diligent is richly supplied." Diligence makes the difference — disciplined activity, which implies consistent obedience. The soul of the lazy person honestly desires fulfillment, maturity, and holiness, yet does not achieve it. This failure arises because he is unwilling to be disciplined and obedient in his Christian life. As a result, the lazy person is characterized by a constant search for shortcuts to achieve the maturity he is craving. The Bible is clear, however, that it is the diligent, disciplined individual who is richly supplied and who will achieve his goals. To know there is no shortcut to maturity can produce a more balanced and realistic Christian life in the undisciplined person.

Step 6: *Limit Excessive Sleep.* The next step is to deal with sleep problems. A person needs to find out how much sleep he really needs and then discipline himself not to get more. This is especially true of the lazy person. As long as he is not ill, regardless of how tired he happens to feel, he should not spend any more time sleeping than he really needs.

Tiredness has a spiraling effect in our lives. When we are tired, we often sin by not doing some necessary activity. Guilt is then produced which, in turn, brings on more tiredness. This increased tiredness makes it all the more likely that we will sin again in a similar way, causing the cycle to occur all over again. When this happens, the way to deal with it is not more sleep, but rather getting back into a disciplined time schedule. When we do this, eventually our perpetual tiredness will go away. Often the problem is taking naps during the day. It is easy to develop a habit of taking a nap in the morning, sitting down to relax after the noon meal, etc. There is a constant resting, folding of hands, sleeping. We can only break this habit by setting a time allotment for sleeping.

Step 7: *Set Realistic Goals.*

> The sluggard buries his hand in the dish, and will not even bring it back to his mouth (Prov. 19:24).

This verse describes the person whose eyes are bigger than his stomach. He reached out for so much he can't even bring it back. The lazy person usually has a problem with unrealistic goals. By setting out to achieve things that cannot be achieved, he always seems to be falling short. This reinforces the frustration and despair in his life. Solutions are quickly achieved when these individuals have help to see what was and what wasn't realistic in their goals. What are realistic goals? This is something you must determine independently. What is realistic for one person might be unrealistic for someone else.

Step 8: Have Hope. There is no reason for despair to reign in a lazy person's life. There really is hope for change for a person who has a habit-level problem of laziness. Hope is necessary to achieve victory. I'd like to turn your attention to Hebrews 6:11,12:

> And we desire each one of you to show the same earnestness in realizing the full assurance of *hope* until the end, *so that* you may not be sluggish, but imitators of those who through faith and patience inherit the promises (RSV).

These verses show us a direct relationship between hope and laziness. Hope is the key to preventing an ongoing sluggishness, which is laziness. In these verses hope is focused on God's promises about our future hope in Christ. I am sure, however, that the relationship holds true for God's promises in general. Hope of solution because God promises it is an essential ingredient in overcoming the problem of laziness. Hope is basic to victory.

There it is. Laziness is sin. Perhaps the person you are discipling has problems he thinks stem from a personality trait of being undisciplined. If so, he probably has a root problem of laziness. Knowing the signs arising out of this sin should help you detect the presence of such laziness. The Bible clearly charts definite steps that you can take in your own life and use in working with someone else to deal with this habit-level problem of laziness.

Notes

[1]Materials on how to have devotions can be found at a local Christian bookstore, or see suggestions in:

> Kuhne, *Dynamics of Personal Follow-up,* pp. 154-59

Study aids for devotional times:

> Bill Bright, *Transferable Concepts* (Arrowhead Springs, Calif.: Crusade for Christ, 1971).

> Mrs. Charles E. Cowman, *Streams in the Desert,* Vol. 1,2 (Grand Rapids: Zondervan, 1965,1966).

> M. R. DeHaan, *Our Daily Bread Favorites* (Grand Rapids: Zondervan, 1971).

> *Design for Discipleship* (Colorado Springs: Navigators, 1973).
> C. H. Spurgeon, *Morning and Evening* (Grand Rapids: Zondervan, 1955).

[2]For further study on evangelism, see:

> Howard Hendricks, *Say It With Love* (Wheaton, Ill.: Victor, 1972).

> Paul Little, *How to Give Away Your Faith* (Downers Grove, Ill.: Inter-Varsity Press, 1966).

Also see:

> Kuhne, *Dynamics of Personal Follow-up,* "A Personal Worker's Suggested Bookshelf," p. 208.

4

Developing a
Discerning Disciple

> But solid food is for the mature, who by constant use
> have trained themselves to distinguish good from
> evil (Heb. 5:14).

Several years ago I was working with a college student
who had recently become a Christian. He was interested in
follow-up and came to nearly every Bible study available.
Unfortunately he became a Christian near the end of the
school year, and shortly after his conversion he left campus to return home for the summer. Upon his return to
campus the following fall, I knew instantly something had
happened to his spiritual life. In tears he explained to me
how he had been drawn into a Bible study group in his
home area and was exposed to much bad teaching. In a
short time he had become hopelessly confused about his
faith and was on the verge of shelving his commitment to
Christ. Why did this happen?

Recently I counseled with a layman who attended an
evangelism training program at which I taught. He became

excited about his faith and had a tremendous burden to share it with others. He went to his pastor, shared his burden, and found the pastor receptive to a witnessing emphasis in his church. Overjoyed, he let the pastor organize and lead a training program for visitation in his church. As the training progressed, however, his joy turned to misgivings. Somehow he didn't agree with what the pastor was saying. The pastor downplayed the role of sin and repentance and seemed to reduce the gospel to simply living a good life. Why did this communication problem exist?

I once knew of a college student, who was a relatively new Christian. He decided it would be good to go to the student foundation maintained on his campus by his denomination. He wanted to see what programs were being offered and if he could assist their work in any way. The chaplain graciously received him and listened intently as he shared how his life changed when he received Christ and the new life he was living since that time. When he finished, the chaplain began to laugh. He then began to tear apart what the new Christian said point by point. He openly ridiculed the idea of conversion and even denied the atoning work of Christ. The student was shattered and disillusioned. Why did they differ so drastically?

These three situations are representative of countless others I could relate to you. They graphically show the need to develop mature disciples. This need is the developing of spiritual discernment. That this is both a legitimate and scriptural goal for disciple-building is clear from the following passages:

> But solid food is for the mature, who by constant use have trained themselves to *distinguish* good from evil (Heb. 5:14).
>
> Then we will no longer be infants, tossed back and forth by the waves, and blown here and there by every

> wind of teaching and by the cunning and craftiness of men in their deceitful scheming (Eph. 4:14).
>
> Dear friends, do not believe every spirit, but *test the spirits* to see whether they are from God, because many false prophets have gone out into the world (1 John 4:1).
>
> Jesus answered: "Watch out that no one deceives you" (Matt. 24:4).

It is extremely important to guard a growing Christian against error in teaching, emphasis, or activities. Because we are creatures of extremes, it is natural for us to head in that direction. We must work to counteract this tendency. There are four basic objectives to strive after when seeking to develop a discerning disciple. They are as follows:

1. Learn to Think Systematically
2. Learn to Examine Presuppositions
3. Learn to Detect Definitions of Terminology
4. Learn to Balance Extremes

Let's examine each of these objectives in more detail.

1. Learn to Think Systematically

Every maturing Christian should develop the habit of thinking systematically. He should seek the interrelatedness of teachings, always striving to discover implications in what is being taught. For example, an attack on the deity of Christ by a Jehovah's Witness affects not only that issue, but also one's understanding of the Atonement. A substitutionary, vicarious death on the cross only makes sense if Jesus was really God. Developing this type of clear searching for the interrelatedness of teachings is a good help in developing a discerning disciple.

2. Learn to Examine Presuppositions

The second objective for developing discernment is to learn to examine the presuppositions of what is being taught or emphasized. False presuppositions will never lead to a true system of thought. The best example I know is Jay Adams' penetrating analysis of secular schools of psychological thought.[1] This type of examination of pre-suppositions is also necessary when it comes to analyzing teachings of cultists, teaching techniques, plans for church renewal, mission strategies, etc. Another example of this type of discernment is found in the writings of Francis Schaeffer, as he examines the presuppositions behind various philosophies of life in the twentieth century.[2]

3. Learn to Detect Definitions of Terminology

A discerning disciple learns to detect the definitions of terminology employed. Perhaps the most important area for this type of discernment is in dealing with cult groups. Often a cult will use a word you understand, but define it in a different way. If you are not aware of the differing definition, it is not immediately apparent that their teachings are wrong. The problem of definitions is also seen in the neo-orthodox and liberal elements of the Christian church. Often they use traditional terminology but strip the meaning from it until it becomes merely a symbol.

4. Learn to Balance Extremes

The final objective for developing discerning disciples is to teach them to balance extremes. When trying to discover the truth about something, it is good to know the opposite extremes. The truth is generally somewhere in the middle. By such an examination of extremes, a much broader picture of the total issue is found. This broadened perspective in turn produces a greater sensitivity to the truth of an issue.

These objectives should be constantly worked toward in your ministry of disciple-building. The Christian with whom you are working must develop the discernment to keep out of extremes and errors. At this point let's turn our attention to some practical areas needing discernment in the growing Christian's life.

AN OBJECTIVE VS. A SUBJECTIVE FAITH

The first area of discernment to be examined deals with the content of the gospel message. Is our faith to be based on an objective or subjective foundation? In other words, is the content or the experience most important in our message of salvation? Does it really matter *what* we believe, or does it only matter *that* we believe? Your disciple is bound to run into proponents of each side, therefore, he must be firmly grounded before he faces the issue.

There are many people today who look upon Christianity as a "leap of faith." Initially the liberals, and later the neo-orthodox teachers, taking their cue from Kierkegaard, abandoned the logical, revealed content of the gospel and stressed the existential element in the gospel. They taught that it wasn't so important what you believed, or even that your belief made sense. It was only important that you "believed." You were saved by your faith, not by the object of your faith. In essence, faith in faith was stressed.

More recently, I have discovered some in the evangelical camp stressing belief without content. Sin, repentance, Lordship, and so on, are never mentioned; and people are challenged to have an existential experience with Christ. I am convinced that real discernment is needed to guard against such error. There is indeed an existential experience of new life in salvation, but only as a by-product of a personal commitment of trust and obedience based on an acceptance of the facts of the gospel. Christianity is based on content. Our acceptance with God is based on what Christ accomplished objectively, in space and time, on the cross. We appropriate that acceptance by an act of repentance and faith.

True discernment is needed among evangelicals

today to make sure that the evangelism that is done is not contentless. Not long ago, while at a youth conference, I heard and evaluated an evangelist who spoke. He spent forty-five minutes talking about the need we have to find answers to the problems we face in our lives. Everyone was listening intently and identifying. He finished by saying that Christ was the answer and challenged people to come forward and "sell out" to Jesus. That was all he said. There was no mention of sin, the Cross, the Resurrection, or repentance. Coming forward in that meeting was no indication of salvation unless people had heard the gospel previously somewhere else. They certainly didn't hear it from that evangelist. By stressing experience at the expense of content, we are dangerously close to conforming to the prevailing existentialism of our day.

A discernment of objective vs. subjective faith is also needed when it comes to growing in Christ. It is crucial that a Christian learn and obey the Word of God. A Christian's obedience is based on objective commands from God, not a subjective sense of leading. This is the mistake I find often arising in periphery groups in Christianity. I have heard many say that they didn't need to study the Bible since the Holy Spirit was all they needed for guidance and living a life that is pleasing to God. This is subjectivism in the worst sense. This emphasis is surely far removed from the biblical emphasis as seen in the following verses:

> Like newborn babes, long for the pure milk of the word . . . (1 Peter 2:2 NASB).

> Do your best to present yourself to God as one approved, . . . and who correctly handles the word of truth (2 Tim. 2:15).

> Thy word is a lamp to my feet and a light to my path (Ps. 119:105).

The growing Christian obeys the objective commands

of God, not merely a subjective sense of leading. In working with the growing Christian, be sure to develop a discernment in these things: (1) be sure he is alert to the *content* of evangelism, and (2) be sure he understands the role of objective obedience. This will do much to stabilize him in his faith.

UNDERSTANDING JUSTIFICATION

The second area of discernment to be examined closely relates to the previous discussion. A growing believer must understand the doctrine of justification, particularly the difference between imputed vs. imparted righteousness.

It is unfortunate, but true, that many Protestants have forgotten the key issue of the Reformation. Does our justification result from imputed or imparted righteousness? To phrase the question differently, Is our acceptance with God based on an internal change or an external identification with Christ? Freedom from the tyranny of the subjectivism inherent in an imparted-righteousness viewpoint was one of the blessings bestowed on the church as a product of the Reformation. To turn our eyes from ourselves to Christ to find assurance of salvation is an important thing in our Christian experience. The Bible clearly shows this position to be the truth. In addition to the clear teachings of Romans 3–5, examine the following verses:

> God made him who had no sin to be sin for us, so that in him we might become the righteousness of God (2 Cor. 5:21).

> And be found in him, not having a righteousness of my own that comes from the law, but that which is through faith in Christ — the righteousness that comes from God and is by faith (Phil. 3:9).

There are two practical reasons why this Reformation

distinction must be seen. First, our assurance of salvation and eternal life was meant to be based on the objective base of the atonement of Christ, something totally outside of ourselves. Second, our focus is inevitably shifted from the *content* of the gospel when we look at internal change rather than external justification. For the serious discipler, further reading is helpful at this point to gain perspective on this issue.[3]

BAD HERMENEUTICS

The third important area for developing discernment in your disciple is in biblical hermeneutics. Hermeneutics is the science of biblical interpretation. Specifically, it sets down the rules that must be followed for a sound interpretation of the Bible. A complete discussion of these rules is beyond the scope of this book; however, there are certain basic principles that any growing Christian should know to guard against misusing God's Word.

1. The Bible Is a Progressive Revelation

A basic rule in understanding the Bible is to understand that it is a progressive revelation. This means that God increasingly revealed a more complete picture of His truth and purposes over time. Thus, the newer the revelation, the more complete our understanding of the truth. This doesn't mean the earlier revelation was wrong, but only that it was less complete. This in turn shows us that many things one time commanded could be overruled in newer revelation because a better picture of truth could be attained.

From this principle we gain two rules. First, the Old Testament is to be understood in light of the New Testament. This does not mean the Old Testament does not make sense alone, but rather the New Testament is the fulfillment of the Old. Thus the New Testament does away with the Old Testament sacrificial, ceremonial, and dietary systems by showing the true reason for them in Jesus

Christ. In spite of the Old Testament commands, we are free from their restrictions because of New Testament teachings. This principle guards against many errors in cults.

The second rule growing from this principle is that the Gospels and Acts are interpreted by the Epistles. That is to say, the Epistles give a detailed explanation to truths lived or alluded to in the Gospels and Acts. This means if we are confused by something in the Gospels or Acts, we ought to check on what the Epistles have to say about the issue.

2. Context Determines Meaning

It is important to know the context before we can understand the meaning of a verse. Is the verse in context written to Christians or non-Christians? Is it referring to growth or salvation? We must answer these questions, for we have no right to use a passage for any reason other than the one for which it was intended.

Knowing this rule guards us against many errors. To always look at context prevents us from drawing wrong conclusions for a passage. It also prevents us from using a verse in an unwarranted way. Without this rule, you could make the Bible say whatever you want it to say. Cults often break this rule, but they don't hold a monopoly on its misuse.

In reviewing a student's message a professor commented, "Right message, wrong text." In essence, he was summarizing this rule. Sometimes we can discern the truth of a verse because it is taught elsewhere, but we will not always be so lucky. We must be aware of context.

3. Important Truths Are Not Hidden

This rule underscores the fact that the major doctrinal truths of our faith are plainly seen in the Scriptures and often repeated throughout the Bible. To know that the important truths will not be hidden in obscure passages or figures of speech will make a disciple much more discerning about the teaching he receives. It certainly will prevent him from majoring on minors.

Many people spend their time trying to read between the lines in the Scriptures because they are convinced that God is trying to hide His truth from all but the wisest and most diligent seeker. Christians must realize that God's purpose in revelation is to *reveal*, not *conceal*. The Scriptures are not a clever puzzle, but rather the Bread of Life to those who will simply study them.

Although Scripture contains metaphors, parables, and figures of speech, the basic foundation for our faith is not hidden in such areas. Plainly literal, didactic portions of Scripture provide the basis for the orthodox faith. An objective study of such passages will yield a growing stability in the life of the Christian who carries out such a study. To understand that the Scriptures are not hiding God's truth will protect the disciple from becoming too mystical in his interpretations of the Word. We must focus our attention on what a passage is literally saying.

Further study in hermeneutics is well worth the time it takes.[4] Remember, we are commanded to "rightly divide" the Word of Truth.

DETECTING CULTS

The fourth major area requiring special discernment on the part of your disciple is the detection of cults. With the proliferation of small study groups and the large increase in new cults, it is crucial that growing Christians know how to detect cult groups. It is no longer sufficient just to identify the four or five major cults and caution growing Christians against contact with such groups. The following are danger signs to be alert to.

Danger Sign 1: Break With Historic Church

The first danger sign is when a group or individual

begins to break with the established church. This doesn't mean breaking fellowship with a specific congregation, but rather with the traditional church at large. Generally a cult group believes the church is apostate and they are God's faithful remnant left on earth. Whenever this tendency becomes apparent in a group, it probably is a cult group.

Danger Sign 2: Majoring on Minors

The second danger sign occurs when a group begins to major on minors — when a particular doctrine, unrelated to salvation, becomes the test of "orthodoxy" and commitment. The literature of the group seems concentrated on minor and obscure truths. An elaborate system of doctrine is often developed, built around obscure verses. This is usually characteristic of cults. If you sense these emphases occuring in a group you attend, be cautious.

Danger Sign 3: Bible Is Not Sole Authority

The third danger sign is an undue emphasis on a book other than the Bible. Usually such a book is considered to be inspired and with validity equal to the Bible. This extra-biblical authority is nearly always a characteristic of a cult. If you find this emphasis, depart from the group.

Danger Sign 4: Bad Christology

Another danger sign is a denial of either the humanity or deity of Christ. A group's orthodoxy is primarily determined by its view of Christ. Any teaching that seems to betray either the humanity or deity of Christ, or questions His uniqueness in some way, is to be suspect. Quickly disassociate with such a group.

Danger Sign 5: Salvation By Works

The fifth danger sign is a denial of salvation by faith. A cult generally emphasizes some type of works-oriented salvation, either in doctrine or practice. Any group that tampers with the meaning of the gospel is immediately suspect. Great discernment is needed in all of this.

My purpose is not to present what different cults teach, but rather to show some danger signs to be alert to. To study the cults would require several whole books and is clearly beyond the scope of this discussion.[5] The most important protection you can give a disciple is to help him gain a solid doctrinal foundation. This will alert him in the best way to detecting cults.

DETECTING UNSOLID PASTORS

The last major area I will discuss which needs special discernment on the part of the growing disciple is the detecting of unsolid pastors. It is often difficult for a new Christian to find out where a pastor really stands. By re-defining content and the use of God-words, a new Christian can be totally misled by a pastor away from biblical teaching. It is important, therefore, to instill in your disciple the type of discernment necessary to solve this problem. The following are issues that should aid in clarifying where a pastor really stands.

Does the pastor teach from the Bible? This is the obvious place to begin. Does the pastor teach from the Bible, or does he merely use it as a formalized part of the service? Are the messages unrelated to Scripture and its claims on our lives? In many cases, the amount the Bible is used is a good indicator of where a man really stands. Another point to consider are the hermeneutics being employed by the pastor. See the prior discussion for help at this point.

Does the pastor believe the Bible to be inspired by God? Many unsolid pastors believe this Book to be *inspiring,* but not inspired. Find out if the pastor in question accepts the Bible as a whole, or if he picks and chooses what to believe. Does he believe the words are inspired or only the concepts? The key is whether the pastor accepts a verbal, plenary inspiration view of Scripture. I often ask a pastor outright whether he accepts this position, which in general, is the position of the orthodox, evangelical pastor.

Does the pastor believe in the Trinity? This question doesn't mean the word *trinity*, but rather the biblically revealed truth of the Triune God. Does the pastor accept the Deity of Christ? Does the pastor believe in the virgin birth, life, death, physical resurrection, and ascension into heaven of Christ? The answers to these questions will certainly begin to reveal a man's true position.

Does the pastor believe in Jesus Christ as the only way to be saved? Have him define salvation for you and how it is to be achieved. Is the emphasis on personal trust and acceptance of Jesus Christ as Savior and Lord? Or is it basically that living a good life is all that is necessary? A pastor's answers to these questions will definitely label him.

If this type of questioning is pursued, a pastor's true position should be revealed. If it turns out that this pastor is not solid, begin to counsel the new Christian about changing churches.

CONCLUSION

Developing discernment is a necessary part of disciple-building. Encouraging a growing Christian to think systematically, examine presuppositions, detect definitions, and balance extremes will contribute greatly to his stability in the faith. Pray for wisdom in this very important undertaking.

Notes

[1]Adams, *Christian Counselor's Manual*, pp. 71–97.

[2]Francis Schaeffer, *Escape From Reason* (Downers Grove, Ill.: InterVarsity Press, 1968).

[3]Read sections on "justification" in the following:

> Louis Berkhof, *Systematic Theology* (Grand Rapids: Eerdmans, 1946).
>
> J. Oliver Buswell, *A Systematic Theology of the Christian Religion*, Vol. II (Grand Rapids: Zondervan, 1972).
>
> Lewis Sperry Chafer, revised by John Walvoord, *Major Bible Themes* (Grand Rapids: Zondervan, 1974).
>
> John Stott, *Basic Christianity* (Grand Rapids: Eerdmans, 1957).
>
> Henry Thiessen, *Introductory Lectures in Systematic Theology* (Grand Rapids: Eerdmans, 1949).

[4]An excellent book on this topic is Bernard Ramm, *Protestant Biblical Interpretation* (Grand Rapids: Baker, 1970).

[5]Suggested reading on the cults:

> Ronald Enroth, *Youth, Brainwashing and the Extremist Cults* (Grand Rapids: Zondervan, 1977).
>
> Anthony Hoekema, *The Four Major Cults* (Grand Rapids: Eerdmans, 1963).
>
> Walter R. Martin, *The Kingdom of the Cults*, rev. ed. (Minneapolis: Bethany Fellowship, 1968).
>
> William Petersen, *Those Curious New Cults* (New Canaan, Conn.: Keats, 1973).
>
> Fritz Ridenour, *So What's the Difference?* (Glendale, Calif.: Regal, 1967).

Developing an Organized Disciple

> Look carefully then how you walk, not as unwise men
> but as wise, making the most of the time . . . (Eph.
> 5:15,16a RSV).

In the development of disciples, one of the key issues that must be dealt with is time management. A growing Christian will soon run into time conflicts as he begins to be presented with more activities than he has time to accomplish. In fact, all Christians who are serious about following Christ as Lord soon find that the possible activities far outweigh the time available to do them.

There seems to be an unwritten principle operating in Christian circles. If a person is committed, then give him an increasing amount to do, up to and beyond the point of breaking. The thinking is that if you are committed and there is a job that needs to be done, then God wants you to do that job. How tragic this becomes. Since when is need the sole criterion for determining God's will? I have found that the perceptive Christian will soon sense more need than he could ever possibly deal with. Is there some objective way of determining the activities that we involve ourselves in?

Early in my Christian life, I faced the same problems. As I became aware of the needs around me, I began to try to meet them. The titles Sunday school teacher, Bible study leader, discipler, evangelist, and so on, began to be tacked behind my name. Soon there came a point of no return and I arbitrarily stopped doing certain activities. Yet I felt terribly guilty for not doing all I had been doing and letting crying needs go unmet.

My counseling room is often filled with those suffering from similar problems. Usually a Christian handles the problem of overactivity in one of two ways. Some just arbitrarily stop doing certain activities. This was the option I took. Unfortunately this way of dealing with the problem results in much guilt over dropped activities. The second option often taken is to keep trying to do more than is humanly possible. The effects of this option are physical breakdowns, family conflicts, and loss of joy in Christian living. This is obviously not what God intends for us to do. How then can we use our time more effectively and choose between activities in the right way?

Time problems can arise from various sources (later in this chapter I'll focus on the most common ones), yet I have found that by far the most common source is the failure of Christians to arrive at priorities for their lives. Not only is establishing priorities important for solving time problems, but is the only objective way of dealing with the issue of what activities to get involved with. There is a working relationship between time management and established priorities, a relationship I will explore a bit later on in the chapter.

The choices facing a Christian regarding which activities to get involved in are far from easy. When the choice is between a good activity or a sinful one, the choice is easy (although the carrying through of the choice might be difficult). Unfortunately, many of the problems faced by the Christian revolve around choices between two good activities. For example, if you only have one evening left in the week, should you lead a Bible study, do visitation, clean the church, or spend time with your family? These types of choices are perplexing to the Christian and can only be solved by using priorities.

Priorities help in developing a life pleasing to God only when this major prerequisite has been met: A person must be in right relationship to God. He must be seeking first His kingdom.

> But seek first his kingdom and his righteousness, and all these things will be given to you as well (Matt. 6:33).

This verse stresses this prerequisite as fundamental to all things. It involves a person's response to salvation and ongoing response to the lordship of Christ. It is impossible to work on priorities until this issue is settled. A person will not experience the peace, joy, and assurance of a life pleasing to God if this basic issue is not clear, in spite of working on other priorities. In fact, the idea of lordship of Christ is the biggest priority of all. Once settled, the following discussion of priorities should prove to be of practical help to the growing Christian you are seeking to disciple.

STEPS FOR ARRIVING AT PRIORITIES

The following discussion of priorities focuses on two things: (1) the establishment of priorities, and (2) the use of priorities in solving time conflicts. The development of these two points is accomplished by following a series of steps.

Step 1: Distinguish Between Commands and Application

As a person begins to read the Word of God, he is immediately struck with the fact that God commands His children to do certain things. Some of His commands are for a limited group of people and for a limited period of time. There are others, however, which are universal in their application. When the Bible presents a universal command, it automatically becomes a priority and we are left with no choice. The following are examples of such universal commands:

1. Sharing your faith (Acts 1:8; 2 Cor. 5:18–20)
2. Worship God, fellowship with believers (Heb. 10:25)
3. Prayer (Phil. 4:6,7)
4. Study of Word (2 Tim. 2:15)

There is much wisdom in studying Scripture to see what God requires of you. When you come upon such universal commands, note whether a certain type of activity is specified. Often there is much leeway in determining how to follow or implement the command. To recognize this is a helpful step in arriving at priorities. This enables you to determine what activities you have a choice over and which ones you don't.

Such an understanding will tell you when you must be involved in some activity to fulfill the command. That no specific activity is mentioned does not mean that you have a choice about *obeying* the command. It only means you have a choice in the *way* to obey it. Perhaps some examples of this principle would be helpful.

God expressly commands that we worship Him and fellowship with other Christians. He does not command how or when we do this. Thus we have no choice but to worship Him and fellowship with other believers, but we do have a choice about when and how. Attending a Sunday evening service is an application of such a command.

We are not commanded to go to Sunday evening church. Perhaps this is a good application of the command, but it is only an application. If, however, we choose not to go to Sunday evening service, we must come up with an alternate activity to implement the command.

Another example of this principle would be Sunday school. God commands that we raise our children in a godly way and teach them about the faith (see Deuteronomy 6, Proverbs, etc.). A way of implementing this command would be the Sunday school program. God does not, however, command that we go to Sunday school or teach it; Sunday school is an optional application of the command to teach our children. If, however, we choose not to utilize Sunday school as a means of applying God's command, we must seek an alternate means of application. God's command must be obeyed, and it is a priority.

A final example would be a church visitation program. God commands that we share our faith. An application of this command is for the church to organize an outreach night where members go out into the community, visit, and evangelize. God does not, however, command you to get involved in such a visitation program. You must, however, determine another way to share your faith if you choose not to do it through this particular program.

We must know what God commands and thus where priorities are established. We must also know when we have an option about application of such commands. Being clear on these issues is a first step to begin to deal with the load of false guilt often heaped on Christians by well-meaning, but misguided people.

Many of God's universal commands relate to attitudes or morality. A knowledge of those commands that imply activity that is of assistance in setting priorities. I recommend that a person develop a list of such commands and

101

79964

begin to think of his involvements in light of the preceding discussion. Such a list will do much to rid the Christian of many unnecessary feelings of guilt or reponsibility.

Step 2: Determine Your Gifts

The second step in determining priorities is to discover your gifts. You were born with certain natural talents or abilities. At conversion the Holy Spirit distributed to you one or more spiritual gifts. Both the natural and spiritual gifts are part of God's sovereign plan for your life. In His wisdom, God gave you these gifts to equip you to perform His perfect will for your time on earth.

God commands that we be faithful in the stewardship of His gifts to us. These gifts include both our natural talents and our spiritual gifts. Thus the effective utilization of these gifts becomes an immediate priority in the life of a Christian. This means that one of the determinations we must make about the activities we are involved in, or considering involvement in, is to find whether our gifts will be utilized or lie dormant in such an activity. See this emphasis on good stewardship in the following verses:

> Each one should use whatever spiritual gift he has received to serve others, faithfully administering God's grace in various forms (1 Peter 4:10).
>
> Now it is required that those who have been given a trust must prove faithful (1 Cor. 4:2).
>
> Having gifts that differ according to the grace given to us, let us use them (Rom. 12:6 RSV).
>
> Every good and perfect gift is from above, coming down from the Father . . . (James 1:17).

In addition to the above verses, Matthew 25:14–30 contains the parable of the talents, where an obvious emphasis is on faithfulness in utilizing the gifts God has given us. The main point here is to realize that because

God commands us to be good stewards of His gifts, the activities that utilize our gifts automatically become priorities for us over those that don't. Learn to evaluate your activities in light of your gifts and the effective utilization of them.[1]

Step 3: Determine Secular Activities Over Which You Have No Choice

The third step focuses on the determination of secular activities over which there is really no choice to make. It is important to see that there are certain things we must do and hence no choice is left. This list is quite small; there are few absolutely essential things. Working is an example of such an activity. It is necessary that man work to earn the money to provide for his personal needs and the needs of his family. A certain portion of the week is thus exempt from the determination of priorities. The classes and studies of a student and the household chores of the homemaker and mother are other examples of secular activities that must be done.

Other examples of this category would be eating and sleeping. These activities must be done and are a necessary time drain in the life of a Christian. There is a question of time duration involved here, however. It is possible to spend too much time doing such necessary activities. This issue will be explored further under step 5 in arriving at priorities.

Step 4: Accept the Biblical Order of Priority Categories

The next step in developing priorities is to understand the general order of importance given to various categories of activities in Scripture. As you study through God's Word, a certain order of priorities becomes evident. Be sure to note these general categories of priorities so that specific activities can be fit into them. The following list shows these categories in order of their importance.

CATEGORY OF PRIORITY	CONTENT OF ACTIVITIES
1	Personal Relationship to God
2	Spiritual/Emotional Family Needs
3	Christian Ministry Activities
4	Vocational Activities
5	All Other Activities

Fig. 3 Biblical Priority Categories

When it comes to deciding between conflicts in your activities, knowing which categories the activities fall into solves the conflict. In cases of conflict, lower priority categories of activities must give way to higher priority categories. Notice this is not a moral judgment on the relative goodness of an activity. Rather it is an objective way to solve conflicts between activities based on an acceptance of biblical priorities.

How did I arrive at the order of priority activities listed? The first category is easy to defend. As was already discussed, Matthew 6:33 clearly places the highest priority on one's personal relationship to Christ. Hence those activities indispensible to achieving this relationship are of highest priority in a Christian's life.

An important point to interject at this place in the discussion is this: *Higher priority activities do not necessarily require more time than lower priority activities; they just take precedence over them.* Actually, the lower priority activities often take more actual time during any given week. For example, your job takes at least forty hours a week, yet is lower in priority than your personal relationship to Christ which takes probably less than ten hours a week. More will be stated on this issue in step 6.

The second category of priority activities is your family. I am sure eyebrows will be lifted when I place this above your Christian ministry activities, yet I am convinced this is the biblical position. I am not saying that your ministry is unimportant, or even necessarily in conflict with your family responsibilities. What I am saying is that in cases of conflict, your family takes priority. I feel this is the only way to understand the many commands of Scripture regarding family responsibility.

I have found that in cases where the family was lowered in priority, those Christians would never argue that the Bible supported their position. Rather, they felt God was exempting them from obeying His commands to fulfill some aspect of His will. This line of reasoning is faulty at two points. First, it makes no sense to think that God wants us to be disobedient to His will as it is revealed in His Word in order to become obedient to a subjective sense of His call. God is immutable and not contradictory. Second, the only real check we have on knowing whether we are following God's perfect will is to see what He has already revealed in His Word about the issue at hand. It is extremely dangerous and foolhardy to think God has exempted you from obedience to His express will. This issue of the importance of the family has been dealt with effectively by others.[2]

There is no question that Christian ministry activities are important and priority must be given them. Of course, step 2 has much bearing on determining which activities to involve yourself in. As stated earlier, your vocation is an activity over which you have no choice and thus is a legitimate time demand on your life. The final category of priority activities is a catch-all for listing those activities that don't fit into the other four.

Once you understand the general order of biblical

priorities and accept them, you are ready to move on to the next step in the development of priorities.

Step 5: Add Specific Activities to General Order of Priorities

Step 5 in the process of priority development is to add specific activities to the general order of priorities discussed in step 4. This is the first movement toward the application of settled priorities to activities and time. Use a separate sheet of paper for each category and begin to fill in each page with specific activities. To accomplish this step, first write down the activities you are presently doing; next add the activities you are thinking about beginning; then add the activities you might do if time would ever allow it; finally add the activities you feel God would have you start. Obviously you will have more activities than time allows in a week. This presents no problem, for in another step you will begin to weed out the activities that are not necessary for you. The list you develop will begin to look similar to the list in Figure 4, except you will have separate pages for each category.

Of course, Figure 4 is not a complete list of activities, yet it should help you list on paper what you are, or want to be, doing in your life. After such a list has been made, you are ready to move into the next step in developing priorities. (See chart on next page.)

Step 6: Determine Time Demands for Each Activity

Step 6 adds the dimension of time to the priority issues. We must be realistic and think through the minimum time demands of the various activities necessary to successfully do such activities. By setting a time demand that is too little or too much, the development of a

CATEGORY OF PRIORITY	CONTENT OF ACTIVITIES	SPECIFIC ACTIVITIES
1	Personal Relationship to God	1. Daily time of prayer/Bible study 2. Weekly worship 3. Read Christian literature 4. Etc.
2	Spiritual/Emotional Family Needs	1. Daily time with wife 2. Daily time with children 3. Family devotions 4. Weekly family night 5. Etc.
3	Christian Ministry Activities	1. Fellowship 2. Teach Sunday school class 3. Visit elderly 4. Group prayer meeting 5. Etc.
4	Vocational Activities	1. Travel time to work 2. Time at work 3. Reading/study for job improvement 4. Etc.
5	All Other Activities	1. Wash car 2. Watch T.V. 3. Grocery shopping 4. Secular reading 5. Etc.

**Fig. 4 Listing Specific Activities Under
General Order of Priorities**

time schedule would be impossible. Time demands of such activities should be determined in light of both a weekly and daily demand. The following form illustrates this principle in action.

CATEGORY	SPECIFIC ACTIVITIES	TIME REQUIREMENTS	
		PER DAY	PER WEEK
1	1. Daily time of prayer and Bible study 2. Weekly worship 3. Read Christian literature	30 minutes	3½ hours 2 hours 4 hours
2	1. Time with wife 2. Time with children 3. Etc.	1 hour 30 minutes	7 hours 3½ hours
3	1. Fellowship 2. Visit elderly 3. Etc.		3 hours 2 hours

Fig. 5

**Time Requirements of Activities
(Partial List)**

Step 7: Circle Essential Activities

The next step in developing priorities is to circle those activities from steps 5 and 6 which are essential. This means those activities over which you have no choice (see previous steps) as well as those you consider to be of highest priority. Spend a good amount of time on this step. Only after you determine these activities can you move on to the next step intelligently.

Step 8: Make a Weekly Schedule

Developing a weekly schedule is the necessary next step in relating the development of priorities to questions of time. A weekly schedule is a tool for using your time more effectively and wisely. Rather than allowing your days to just happen, or trusting your memory to stimulate you to doing priority activities, a weekly schedule puts it all down on paper and enables you to function according to your priorities. Establishing a weekly schedule makes you better able to get the things done that are most important. This tool also enables you to be much more realistic about what you can and can't do at any point in time, a fact indispensible in learning to say no. A time schedule also enables you to spot potential conflicts between projected activities, conflicts that can be solved on the basis of priorities.

A weekly schedule should cover all your waking hours seven days a week. Begin to fill in the weekly schedule with the activities circled in step 7 based on time demands from step 6. Once this has been done, fill in the remainder of time available on the basis of priority. Once the schedule fills up, you can do no more. If the schedule fills up on the basis of priorities, you can feel at peace about doing as much as God desires you to do. You will be able to be much more realistic about what you can and can't do. Since emergencies can occur and throw off your schedule, be sure to leave at least two "time gaps" of several hours each to act as an emergency filler, a place where you can do something the emergency prevented you from doing.

Figure 6 illustrates a sample time schedule. It should be enough to show you how you can develop yours.

Step 9: Live by Priority, Not Pressure

This last step should not be overlooked. The purpose of priorities and scheduling time is to release you from the tyranny of the urgent. I don't believe God wants us to operate under pressure. The fact that something needs to

	SUNDAY	MONDAY	TUESDAY	WEDNESDAY	THURSDAY	FRIDAY	SATURDAY
6 AM							
	GET UP / DEVOTIONS	GET UP / DEVOTIONS	GET UP / DEVOTIONS	GET UP / DEVOTIONS	GET UP / DEVOTIONS	GET UP / DEVOTIONS	GET UP / DEVOTIONS
7—8	GET READY FOR CHURCH / BKFT.	BKFT / TRAVEL TO WORK	BKFT	BKFT	BKFT	BKFT	BKFT WITH FAMILY
8—9		WORK	WORK	WORK	WORK	WORK	
9—10	CHURCH						WORK AROUND HOME
10—11							
11—12							
12—1	LUNCH	LUNCH	LUNCH	LUNCH—BIBLE STUDY AT WORK	LUNCH	LUNCH	LUNCH
1—2		WORK	WORK	WORK	WORK	WORK	
2—3	VISIT WITH FRIENDS						SHOPPING
3—4							
4—5	RELAX WITH FAMILY	TRAVEL HOME	TRAVEL HOME				
5—6		SUPPER AND FAMILY TIME	SUPPER AND FAMILY TIME	SUPPER AND FAMILY TIME	SUPPER AND FAMILY TIME	SUPPER AND FAMILY TIME	SUPPER AND FAMILY TIME
6—7							
7—8		FOLLOW-UP	DO WORK				
8—9	OPEN TIME GAP	AND DISCIPLING APPOINTMENTS	PREPARATION FOR LEADING BIBLE STUDY	FELLOWSHIP GROUP	OPEN TIME GAP	FAMILY NIGHT	TAKE WIFE OUT
9—10							
10—11	READ	TIME WITH WIFE	TIME WITH WIFE	TIME WITH WIFE	TIME WITH WIFE	READ AND BED	
11—12	BED	READ AND BED	READ AND BED	READ AND BED	READ AND BED		BED

Fig. 6   Weekly Schedule

be done doesn't mean you are to do it. Don't succumb to the pressures others place on you. Once you have established priorities and developed a schedule of time usage in light of them, learn to evaluate all new potential activities by this backdrop. A way this might be done is to ask the following questions about each new activity that presents itself: Does this activity fit into my priority structure? Does doing it mean that some higher priority item will have to stop? Should I rework my priorities in light of this new opportunity? Asking such questions will do much to keep priorities in focus as we face choices to make.

Remember that it takes much time and prayer to develop priorities. A careful analysis of your gifts is vitally important. Without this analysis, you really cannot go through steps 5 through 7, because you will have no way of evaluating the types of activities to be involved in. Don't allow others to determine your priorities. You are responsible before God to do this yourself. The counsel of others is helpful, but not authoritative.

The development of a weekly schedule is meant to be a helpful tool, not a straitjacket. Flexibility is possible and definitely not sinful. The exciting thing about following a time schedule consistently is that even when you must break it occasionally, you have been able to do what was of high priority as a pattern of life. Periodic crises then cause no lasting problems. If, however, a person does not follow a schedule consistently, then crises simply put him further behind than ever and prevent even more the accomplishing of God's will.

If, after step 1, you decide a certain activity is not fulfilling the universal commands the way you feel necessary, don't forget to come up with an alternative activity. Otherwise you will end up not doing what God commands you to do. Remember, priorities are not established to get you out of things so much as to put you into the right things.

Finally, it might be helpful to develop a list of things that you will never do under any circumstances. This list should not be made arbitrarily, but rather on the basis of a sound analysis of priorities and gifts. Such a list would do much to help you say no to things you realize God does not want you to do.

MAKING BETTER USE OF TIME

As I stated earlier, time conflicts arise from a variety of sources. Although priorities are a major issue in solving time problems, there are other things to know in making better use of your time. I feel Christians are particularly vulnerable to Satan at the issue of time. If Satan can fool us into making mistakes in this area, he will be successful in dulling our effectiveness in serving Christ. Thus, for the person seeking to disciple others and produce multiplication, time becomes an important issue.

Time, as in the case of gifts, is a stewardship from God. We must be good stewards of it. We must utilize time in a way that accomplishes God's purposes in giving it to us. One question to ask yourself to help pinpoint the issue is: Who controls your time — you, others, or God? Answering this question truthfully will show you whether you are living according to priority or pressure.

There are a number of basic principles which do much to clarify our thinking when it comes to issues of time. My purpose here is not to elaborate on time-management concepts and organizational principles. This has already been done by others. I am interested in pointing out some truths that will crystallize your thinking on the issues of time and the Christian's life before God.

1. *All men are created equal with respect to time.* No one really has any more or any less of it. We all are granted

twenty-four hours a day with which to serve our Lord. The differences between believers arise over *how* we use time, not over *how much* time we have. I often have to remind people of this not-so-obvious-fact. When we don't take this fact of equality into consideration, we are tempted to come up with excuses of less time to cover up our bad time usage.

2. *We will always have enough time to do God's will.* Time problems originate when we seek to do more than God's will for our lives. This principle grows out of the conviction that God doesn't mock us by making His perfect will unachievable. This principle also grows out of the biblical picture of God as a God of peace and no confusion.

> For God is not a God of confusion but of peace (1 Cor. 14:33).

This principle ought to act as a red warning flasher in our minds whenever we find ourselves overwhelmed and unable to accomplish all that we feel responsible for doing. Of course, laziness can also cause time problems, and this issue is dealt with in the third chapter.

3. *Time is lost in the smallest units first.* We lose minutes before we lose hours, days before we lose weeks. As obvious as this principle seems, most people I counsel are missing it. Their focus when dealing with time problems is macroscopic, not microscopic. Much time is wasted because we use the gaps of time between activities in unproductive ways. In an experiment one week, people from various walks of life kept track of the amount of time they needed to wait between activities. This included waiting on appointments, time between classes, waiting to cook supper, and so on. Many of these people found they lost over a dozen hours in a week's time by such time drains. Make it a habit to keep work with you to fill such time gaps. Reading a book or magazine, doing corre-

spondence, knitting, and memorizing Scripture are all examples of what could be done to redeem lost time.

4. *Relaxation is not wasted time.* Relaxation is a necessity for the proper functioning of your body. See this emphasis in the following verse:

> The apostles returned to Jesus, and told him all that they had done and taught. And he said to them, "Come away by yourselves to a lonely place, and rest a while . . ." (Mark 6:30,31 RSV).

The need for rest was clear in the Old Testament teaching on the Sabbath and Sabbath years. God created us in such a way that without rest, our productivity gradually diminishes. We need to have a balance and add periods of relaxation into our schedule.

5. *Time management is a measure of knowing God's will and living a Spirit-filled life.* As the passage on time in Ephesians 5:15–18 clearly points out, time management provides a way of walking carefully before God and of proving His perfect will. Contextually I feel there is no mistake in the fact that being filled with the Holy Spirit is mentioned. I have discovered that my awareness of being empowered by God and being used by Him has been greatest when I knew my time was being used effectively. Conversely, when I was having time problems, my productivity and joy were greatly diminished. May God grant you the wisdom to see the importance of effective use of time in the stewardship of your life.

> *Look carefully then how you walk,* not as unwise men but as wise, *making the most of the time,* because the days are evil. Therefore do not be foolish, but *understand what the will of the Lord is.* And do not get drunk with wine, for that is debauchery; but *be filled with the Spirit* (Eph. 5:15–18 RSV).

Notes

[1]For further reading on this topic, see the following:

William McRae, *The Dynamics of Spiritual Gifts* (Grand Rapids: Zondervan, 1976).

Bob Smith, *When All Else Fails, Read the Directions* (Waco, Tex.: Word, 1975).

Ray Stedman, *Body Life* (Glendale, Calif.: Regal, 1972).

[2]See the following books:

Jay Adams, *Christian Living in the Home* (Grand Rapids: Baker, 1972).

Howard Hendricks, *Heaven Help the Home!* (Wheaton, Ill.: Victor, 1974).

6

Developing a
Biblical Disciple

Do your best to present yourself to God as one approved, a workman who does not need to be ashamed and who correctly handles the word of truth (2 Tim. 2:15).

In any discussion of spiritual leadership and discipleship development, the role of knowledge must be focused upon. It is imperative that a growing Christian gain an increasing command of the Word of God. A man of God must be a man of the Word. It is indispensable. The point of this chapter is to show why this knowledge is so important and to give some practical suggestions on how to begin to achieve this knowledge.

THE NEED FOR BECOMING
A MAN OF THE WORD

Without exception, those who have been mightily used by God were those who knew the Word. Of course, there were other factors in their growth and effectiveness, yet the key role of the Word of God must not be overlooked. Early in my Christian life I began to see the importance of this knowledge. As I began to reach out and share my faith with others, my limited knowledge of God's Word proved a hindrance for me. Often I found myself unable to answer questions about the gospel raised by non-Christians. I also found myself "glued" to following a set presentation of the gospel because I didn't know enough to depart far from it. These experiences greatly motivated me to grow in my knowledge of the Word.

I was further motivated to know the Word better when I saw mature believers use it to meet the needs of other people. When I faced people who were in the midst of crisis situations, I felt totally inadequate to apply the Word of God to their needs. Yet others seemed able to apply the Word to almost any need they faced. And it was an application that resulted in practical help to the people in need. How wonderful it was to begin to be of the same type of help to those in need when I also began to learn the Word in more depth.

There is no question but that the Bible commands a Christian to grow in his knowledge of the Word of God. The following verses stress various commands to know the Word.

1. We are commanded to know God's Word because we need to correctly understand His Word. It is necessary to study to gain the knowledge of His will. Ignorance is never an acceptable excuse to God. God wants our obedience to be specific, not general.

> Do your best to present yourself to God as one approved, a workman who does not need to be ashamed and who correctly handles the word of truth. (2 Tim. 2:15).

2. We are commanded to know God's Word because spiritual growth is impossible apart from it.

> Like newborn babes, long for the pure milk of the word, that by it you may grow in respect to salvation (1 Peter 2:2 NASB).

3. We are commanded to know God's Word because it is our offensive weapon in spiritual warfare. Christ clearly left us this example in His temptations in the wilderness. He dealt with each satanic temptation by repeating Scripture.

> Take the helmet of salvation and the sword of the Spirit, which is the word of God (Eph. 6:17).

4. We are commanded to know the Word of God because we are responsible to deal with error when it arises. Error must be confronted in an objective way. Feelings or speculations are not sufficient when it comes to dealing with error. Error must be dealt with by contrasting it with truth, i.e., the truth of God's Word.

> He must hold firmly to the trustworthy message as it has been taught, so that he can encourage others by sound doctrine and refute those who oppose it (Titus 1:9).

Not only is the Bible clear in commanding that we become students of the Word, but it also devotes much space to answering the question of "why." In the previous verses this was touched on, but I feel it is necessary to expand on this and find out more completely the "whys" of the Bible study. I have discovered that an understanding of why we should study the Bible was of more importance in motivating people than all the exhortative sermons we could hear.

First of all, becoming a student of the Word contributes to our spiritual and mental stability. It helps us to know the mind of Christ and roots us more firmly in our faith. Stability is an important achievement in the Christian life. The following verses clearly show the causal relationship between knowing the Word of

119

God (and resulting doctrine) and stability:

> Then we will no longer be infants, tossed back and forth by the waves, and blown here and there by every wind of teaching and by the cunning and craftiness of men in their deceitful scheming (Eph. 4:14).

> Blessed is the man who walks not in the counsel of the wicked, nor stands in the way of sinners. nor sits in the seat of scoffers; but his delight is in the law of the LORD, and on his law he meditates day and night. He is like a tree planted by streams of water, that yields its fruit in its season, and its leaf does not wither. In all that he does, he prospers (Ps. 1:1–3).

Becoming a student of the Word also produces within us true wisdom. Wisdom has been defined as the ability to make practical applications of truth. Wisdom gives us the ability to see where God's commands meet the fabric of real life. Increasing knowledge of God's Word enables us to become more wise in the issues of life than the most learned, philosophically wise men in the secular world around us. The following verses point up this fact.

> The law of the LORD is perfect, reviving the soul; the testimony of the LORD is sure, making wise the simple; the precepts of the LORD are right, rejoicing the heart; the commandment of the LORD is pure, enlightening the eyes; the fear of the LORD is clean, enduring forever; the ordinances of the LORD are true, and righteous altogether. More to be desired are they than gold, even much fine gold; sweeter also than honey and drippings of the honeycomb. Moreover by them is thy servant warned; in keeping them there is great reward (Ps. 19:7–11).

> Thy commandment makes me wiser than my enemies, for it is ever with me. I have more understanding than all my teachers, for thy testimonies are my meditation. I understand more than the aged, for I keep thy precepts (Ps. 119:98–100).

Becoming a student of the Word greatly increases our victory in the struggle with sin. The Bible does this in several ways. First, it convicts us when we sin. This is important because it is easy to become hard-hearted and dull of hearing when we are sinning. Thus to read the Word and see where we are wrong is a great help. The Bible also spells out how to get back into God's will when we have stumbled. The Word never focuses on the negative alone, but is positive in helping us back on the path. The Bible also shows us how to keep from falling into sin, that is, how to deal successfully with temptations. These are ways that the Word helps us deal with sin. See the following verses:

> I have laid up thy word in my heart, that I might not sin against thee (Ps. 119:11).
>
> All Scripture is God-breathed and is useful for teaching, rebuking, correcting and training in righteousness, so that the man of God may be thoroughly equipped for every good work (2 Tim. 3:16,17).

Becoming a student of the Word gives us hope. Hope is a rich gift that is only available to the believer. But we must never forget our hope is not based on speculations; rather, it grows out of the revealed promises of the Word of God. It is only through study that we gain the knowledge of these promises. The following verses stress this role of the Word:

> And take not the word of truth utterly out of my mouth, for my hope is in thy ordinances. . . . Remember thy word to thy servant, in which thou hast made me hope. This is my comfort in my affliction that thy promise gives me life (Ps. 119:43,49,50).
>
> For everything that was written in the past was written to teach us, so that through endurance and the encouragement of the Scriptures we might have hope (Rom. 15:4).

Becoming a student of the Word gives us peace. As we grow in our understanding of the Bible, we gain an increasing sense of inner peace and stability. This inner sense of peace is basically the sense of peace with God. This peace is sought after by the world but is found only in Christ. I have found that this sense of peace with God is sporadic for those Christians who don't study the Word. The following verse makes this point clear.

> Great peace have those who love thy law; nothing can make them stumble (Ps. 119:165).

Finally, becoming a student of the Word enables us to become adequate to face life and the problems that come with it. Adequacy is a greatly desired dream for most people. To know that you will be adequate to face whatever life dishes out is a gift almost beyond belief. Yet this is exactly what is promised you as a believer who knows the Word. The following verses clearly make this promise seen:

> Now I commit you to God and to the word of his grace, which can build you up . . . (Acts 20:32).

> All Scripture is God-breathed and is useful for teaching, rebuking, correcting and training in righteousness, so that the man of God may be thoroughly equipped for every good work (2 Tim. 3:16,17).

For these and many other reasons, a knowledge of God's Word is indispensable to Christian growth and fruitfulness. All Christians should thus strive to become the students of God's Word that He commands them to be. I trust that the reasons why have been satisfactorily answered. If so, then it is time to press on to the question of "how."

HAVING A TEACHABLE SPIRIT

The first step in becoming a man of the Word is to be sure you have a teachable spirit. Just to read the Bible will avail little if the one reading it does not want to learn. The writer of the Book of Hebrews focuses on the problems resulting from being unteachable:

> About this we have much to say which is hard to explain, since you have become dull of hearing. For though by this time you ought to be teachers, you need some one to teach you again the first principles of God's word. You need milk, not solid food; for every one who lives on milk is unskilled in the word of righteousness, for he is a child. But solid food is for the mature, for those who have their faculties trained by practice to distinguish good from evil (Heb. 5:11–14 RSV).

This passage was written to Christians, in fact, probably to well-educated Christians. The problem was that these Christians had received much information but had done nothing with it. As a result, they had grown dull of hearing (in a spiritual sense) and therefore were unteachable. The result of being unteachable was that they had to go back to the beginning and study the basics all over again. This was necessary in spite of the fact that they had been taught much. This plainly shows that unless a person is teachable, studying will bring about little lasting results. This is a danger we ought to be aware of as disciplers and disciples.

Proverbs 1:28–2:5 is a key passage of Scripture in helping us to know what it means to have a teachable spirit:

> Then they will call upon me, but I will not answer; they will seek me diligently but will not find me. Because they hated knowledge and did not choose the fear of the LORD, would have none of my counsel, and despised all my reproof, therefore they shall eat the fruit of their way and be sated with their own devices. For the simple are killed by their turning away, and the complacence of fools destroys them; but he who listens to me will dwell secure and will be at ease, without dread of evil. My son, if you receive

> my words and treasure up my commandments with
> you, making your ear attentive to wisdom and inclin-
> ing your heart to understanding; yes, if you cry out for
> insight and raise your voice for understanding, if you
> seek it like silver and search for it as for hidden
> treasures; then you will understand the fear of the
> LORD and find the knowledge of God.

This passage focuses first on the results of not having a
teachable spirit, that is, hating knowledge, reproof, etc.
There are certain unavoidable results of an unteachable
spirit. Problems in one's prayer life are unavoidable. A
strong sense of unanswered prayer will be evidenced. A
sense of separation from God is also there. You seek Him
but don't find Him. Rebellion against God's discipline also
characterizes such a problem.[1] In addition to rebelling
against God's discipline, there is a general rebellion
against God. This rebellion can be active or passive. Active
rebellion is shown to be an actual turning away from God
to one's own way. Passive rebellion is identified as complacency. Spiritual complacency is clearly shown in this
passage to be rebellion against God and is an unavoidable
result of having an unteachable Spirit.

So the question remains, What does it mean to have a
teachable spirit? How can we demonstrate this teachableness and avoid the problems identified in the preceding
discussion? This passage in Proverbs identifies eight
characteristics of a teachable spirit. If these characteristics
are followed, teachableness is achieved in the life of a
Christian.

1. *Receive God's Word (2:1a).* This characteristic of a
teachable spirit focuses on the way of approaching the
Word of God. The Hebrew word translated *receive* has the
idea of receiving for the purpose of using. It is inadequate
to approach the Word simply for the purpose of satisfying
your curiosity. It is not enough to study simply for intellec-

tual satisfaction. We must study for the purpose of application. This idea is repeated in Isaiah 29:13,14, where the inadequacy of learning by rote without application is clearly shown.

2. *Treasure Up Commandments (2:1b).* This characteristic of a teachable spirit points up the future benefit of present study. The idea here is to hoard up the Word of God for future use. This doesn't conflict with the first part of the verse because application is still the emphasis, with the added perspective that the Word will be worth remembering for future needs. Our motive for study must not just be to solve an immediate problem, but rather to also be equipped for future needs and problems. We need vision to see the lasting benefits of our study of the Word.

3. *Attentive to Wisdom (2:2a).* This characteristic stresses two distinct aspects of having a teachable spirit. First, the emphasis is on attentiveness. The idea in the Hebrew is to listen closely and seriously. It is impossible to have a teachable spirit when you are only half listening or daydreaming. The Word of God demands your full attention. You must place priority on this study and discipline yourself to be serious in your approach to the Bible. The second aspect deals with wisdom. We are to be attentive to wisdom, that is, paying close attention to the practical applications of the Word of God to life as we find it. Unless we keep an eye on the application of the Word of God, our study becomes purely academic.

4. *Incline Your Heart to Understanding (2:2b).* This characteristic focuses on the idea of reliance. The Hebrew word for *incline* implies the action of turning. This turning is from one object of reliance to another. The key is to learn to trust God's Word rather than your own reasoning to know how to live your life. There needs to be a conscious shifting of reliance from yourself to God in the development of a teachable spirit. It is a difficult step to

turn from our self-sufficiency and humbly rely on God's answers, but there is really no choice for the growing Christian. This idea is stressed clearly in Proverbs 3:5:

> Trust in the LORD with all your heart, and do not rely on your own insight.

5. *Cry Out for Insight (2:3a)*. This characteristic emphasizes the role of prayer in having a truly teachable spirit. The Hebrew word implies calling out by name. We must ask the right person for insight; we must call to God, not to men. Prayer is not meant to be a cliché that sanctifies the topic, but rather is meant to be a foundation for a meaningful time in God's Word. The following verse stresses this idea:

> If any of you lacks wisdom, he should ask God, who gives generously to all without finding fault, and it will be given to him (James 1:5).

6. *Raise Your Voice for Understanding (2:3b)*. This characteristic of a teachable spirit is similar to the last. There is the added idea, however, of a continuing action. Prayer is meant to be an ongoing part of your life. It ought to be consistently utilized in your attempts to study God's Word. Prayer is not meant to be a once-and-for-all act, but rather a process.

7. *Seek It Like Silver (2:4a)*. Here we focus on the priority of and intensity of desire for the Word of God in our lives. The study of God's revelation is meant to be placed high on our priority lists, because the gain from studying it exceeds the gain of finding silver.

> Happy is the man who finds wisdom, and the man who gets understanding; for the gain of it is better than gain from silver and its profit better than gold (Prov. 3:13,14).

This point also stresses intensity of desire. The truly teachable spirit has a burning passion to know God's

Word, and nothing can successfully stand in his way. This idea is also seen in the following verse:

> My soul is consumed with longing for thy ordinances at all times (Ps. 119:20).

8. *Search for It As for Hidden Treasure (2:4b).* This characteristic is similar to the previous one, but includes the idea of ongoing activity. Studying God's Word is a lifelong priority. Growth in wisdom is a process that continues throughout our entire life. We never arrive at a point where we no longer need to study. Never stop too soon in your search.

After clearly identifying the characteristics of a teachable spirit, the passage goes on to identify the results of having such a teachable spirit. Not only are the problems identified at the start successfully overcome, but also two positive benefits result. The teachable spirit gains understanding and knowledge (v. 5). Both of these results are indispensable in becoming a man of the Word.

A man of God must gain understanding, and understanding is synonymous with wisdom. A man of the Word must gain the ability to see the applications of God's Word to life, because God desires doers, not just hearers, of the Word. In order to become a doer of the Word, we must see how it directly applies to our life. Thus, the ability to see where the Word applies to our life and to be obedient in such applications are important aspects of becoming a man of the Word, a biblical disciple. We truly need understanding.

The man of God must also gain knowledge in two distinct areas. First, this knowledge refers to doctrine — the growing Christian needs the objective stability of sound doctrine. Our faith is meant to rest on revelation, not vain babbling and speculation. The data of the Bible provides us with the necessary objective truth to give our lives stability.

Second, this knowledge refers to personally knowing

God. As we study His Word with teachable spirits, we gain the subjective satisfaction of a deepened personal relationship with God. What a fantastic privilege is ours as Christians, to be able to know personally the God who is there, who created us and all the world. To know Him more intimately is the promise of this passage.

PRACTICAL BIBLE STUDY METHODS

Having laid the foundation of the need for becoming a man of the Word, and having examined the need for a teachable spirit, let us examine some practical methods for actually studying the Word of God. Training in the how-to's of Bible study is necessary in motivating a consistent approach to the Word of God.

The single most important factor in training someone in Bible study methods is to keep it simple. Several years ago I trained a group of laymen and college students in a method of inductive Bible study. Many hours were devoted to this endeavor. I was proud of the people who attended faithfully and worked hard to learn the methods. At the end of the course everyone was enthusiastic and sure that the course marked a turning point in their Christian lives. From now on they would become men of the Word.

Several months later I followed up the class with a personal contact with each member. To my astonishment, none of them were continuing to follow the methods they were taught. The most common excuse given was that the methods took so much time they seldom were able to utilize them. This taught me a good lesson. Unless a method is simple, easy to use, and realistic in its time demands, it will not be of much help to those who attend the training. The methods taught in this chapter meet the above criteria. More importantly, they will produce benefits to those who utilize them.

Learning to Systematize

I believe it is fundamental to learn where things are located in the Bible. This spatial knowledge of the Word of God will do much to make it a more useful tool. Some have said that knowing where to look for information is 90 percent of an education. I would agree with this point in regard to the Word of God. I personally feel that knowing where to look for things in the Word is a higher priority in a growing Christian than memorizing Scripture. I don't mean this in an either/or sense, but rather that more time should be spent learning to systematize than memorize.

The initial procedure in systematizing Scripture is to read a particular book of the Bible through twice in its entirety. Once this is done, you will be ready to utilize two simple methods for systematizing the Word. The first focuses on developing book charts, the second on developing book outlines. These two methods will enable you to gain an ever-increasing knowledge of how the Bible is arranged.

1. *Book Chart.* The purpose for developing a book chart is to learn the major content of each chapter in each book of the Bible. The value of this is that a Christian will then gain a growing knowledge of where to turn to answer specific questions and problems. Even when a particular verse reference slips your mind, this knowledge will enable you to turn to related passages and often discover the verse you were after.

Let me give you several examples of the value of knowing the major content of different chapters in the Bible. Perhaps you are teaching someone on the topic of spiritual gifts. A knowledge of chapter content would help you realize that Romans 12, 1 Corinthians 12–14, Ephesians 4, and 1 Peter 4 are chapters that deal with this issue. Turning to these chapters will most often answer any questions you might have. Or perhaps you are dealing with qualifications for spiritual leadership. In this case 1 Timothy 3, Titus 1, and 1 Peter 5 should come to your mind. The method that will help you to gain this type of knowledge is the "book chart."

A book chart simply helps you summarize chapter content into a form that is easy to memorize. The following is a sample of one chapter in such a chart:

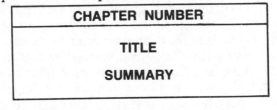

CHAPTER NUMBER
TITLE
SUMMARY

Fig. 7 Single-Chapter Book Chart

The key element of this chart is the chapter summary title. This summary is what you will memorize about the chapter. Thus the title should be brief, but comprehensive. It should bring to mind the major emphasis of the chapter. It should be carefully worded and not so generalized as to confuse you with other chapters in the book or in other books. The following are examples of this type of summary.

Example One: John 1. This chapter focuses on several points: the deity of the Word, the Word becoming flesh, John's witness to the Word, and the calling of several disciples. The title should summarize these ideas and also be concise. This is how I summarized it: "John and Disciples See the Word Become Flesh."

Example Two: John 2. This chapter has two main emphases: first, the miracle at Cana, and second, the first cleansing of the temple. The title should summarize these points clearly. This is how I summarized it: "Wedding Cheered, Temple Cleansed."

Example Three: John 3. This chapter focuses on Jesus' discourse with Nicodemus and the decrease in importance of John's ministry. I summarized this chapter in the following way: "Nicodemus Questions, John Decreases."

There are no right or wrong title summaries. The right one for you is the one which best brings back to your mind the content of the chapter. The titles don't even have to be complete sentences. A chapter summary title should be found for each chapter of a book. The chart for the book should be able to be fit on a single page of 8½" x 11" paper. I have found that by turning a page on its side and making 6 columns across and 4 sets of columns down, nearly every book can be thus summarized. The following is an example of such a chart:

NAME OF BOOK					
1	2	3	4	5	6
TITLE	TITLE	TITLE	TITLE	TITLE	
7	8	9	10	11	12
13	14	15	16	17	18
19	20	21	22	23	24

Fig. 8 Book Chart

After a book chart is developed, the next step is to memorize it. This is relatively easy to do. There is a special benefit from this method as well. When you work to memorize the chart, and continue to review it over time, the riches of a whole book become yours. I have found this method easy and quick enough that most people will use it and consistently grow in their knowledge of the Word.

2. *Book Outline.* The second method for gaining a systematic knowledge of God's Word is the "book outline." The purpose of a book outline is to identify the structure of a book. By this I mean finding out what the major points of a book are and what are supportive points. Identifying the structure enables you to see the contextual development of a book. Without such an understanding of context, we can lose sight of why God said a particular thing. If taken out of context, a passage could well give rise to error. The value of this method is that it will prevent you from majoring on minors and force you to think contextually, thus preventing errors arising by taking verses out of context. The key idea, however, is to see the structural development of a book and begin to understand just why it was written.

The book outline is a simple method of studying the Word. It is nothing more than a major point outline such as would be used when studying any type of literature. As already pointed out, though simple, the outline yields great benefits to those who follow it. The form such an outline follows is seen in Figure 9.

In the development of a book outline, it is important not to become too detailed. It is seldom necessary to go beyond outline points A., B., etc., into subpoints such as 1., 2., a., b. The focus of attention should be on the major points, the purposes for which a book was written. A help in developing such a focus is to write a summary title for a book to show the overall purpose for which it was written. In some cases, the author clearly states it, as in the Gospel of John:

> These are written that you may believe that Jesus is the Christ, the Son of God, and that by believing you may have life in his name (John 20:31).

Other books will not be as easy to determine, yet the effort will greatly reward the student.

BOOK TITLE
Summary of Purpose
I.   Major point (references)
    A. Supportive point (references)
    B. Supportive point (references)
II.   Major point (references)

Fig. 9 Book Outline

In the development of the outline, use complete sentences for each major point and subpoint. Also add the Scripture references for the passage covered by the point. You will soon see that the points don't usually align with the chapters. This is why a book chart alone is inadequate to systematize your understanding of Scripture.

Often a study Bible is a great help in outlining a book. Study Bibles such as the Harper Study Bible, Thompson Chain Reference Bible, New Scofield Reference Bible, and others contain examples of such outlining. Although these outlines are not "inspired," they do help one to think in outline form when approaching the Word of God. It is a good investment to buy one of these study Bibles and begin to use it.

As in the case of the book chart, I have found that a book outline could usually fit on a single page. Once developed and stapled together with the book chart, a person is well on his way toward learning in a systematic way the Word of God.

Learn to Synthesize

I have found it to be extremely helpful in my understanding of God's Word to be able to relate the parts to the whole. The word *synthesize* means to make up by combin-

133

ing the parts. Interrelating different parts of the Word of God provides stability by protecting against extremes. When a point is stressed several times and is not in conflict with what is taught other places, the likelihood of its being correct greatly increases.

There are four basic methods for learning to synthesize: (1) learning to use the marginal references in a good study Bible (2) disciplining yourself to develop your own marginal references, (3) learning to use a concordance, and (4) learning to use a topical Bible. Let's examine each of these in more depth.

1. *Marginal references in a study Bible* are an exceedingly helpful tool for the student of the Word. I would suggest that anyone who is serious about learning the Word of God should buy a good Bible with marginal references. Marginal references are the Bible verses footnoted on the sides, middle, or bottom of the page in a reference Bible. The footnoted verses, or marginal references, direct the student's attention to another part of the Word of God dealing with the same or similar topic.

Marginal references are usually developed in one of two ways. Some reference Bibles use marginal references to direct attention to other verses using the same or similar phrases or words, as in the New American Standard Version, for example. Other reference Bibles operate on a topic reference principle. In this case the marginal references direct attention to verses dealing with the same topic, but not necessarily the same wording. Such topic marginal references are found in the Harper Study Bible, for example.

Whether marginal references are arranged according to phrase or topic, most are developed in a chainlike fashion. This means that the references are like a chain that leads you to more references when you turn to a new passage. This chain design forces you to begin to synthesize in your study of God's Word. It also is fun to explore the reaches of such a chain. An hour can pass before you realize it. The following is an example of such a chain, based on John 3:3, in the Harper Study Bible. The idea being referenced is "born anew." Each marginal reference at a verse is listed, those not pertaining to "born anew" are stopped and not followed further.

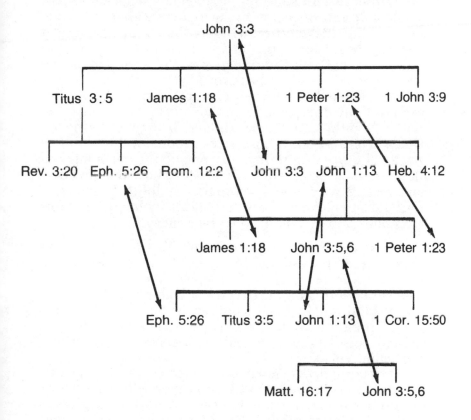

Fig. 10 Marginal References

135

Marginal references are fun to use and edifying as well. They are not, however, exhaustive or inspired. Learn to use them as a helpful study aid in your study of God's Word.

2. *Developing your own marginal references* is the second method of synthesizing. Although a difficult task, it is an excellent discipline to learn. The key to this method is to think in terms of topic references. What other passages of Scripture deal with the topic you are now studying? Asking this question will force you to synthesize. Of course, the ability to use this method increases as your knowledge of God's Word increases. Yet even with newer Christians this method has proved effective.

I have used the development of marginal references as part of my devotions for several years. I am able to integrate synthesizing of Scripture with meditation on God's Word. My devotions have become infinitely more practical since beginning this practice. I encourage all the Christians with whom I work to follow this practice, and most have found it extremely helpful. I have also found it beneficial to use a study Bible with large margins to contain my own additional references.

3. *Using a concordance* is the third method of synthesizing. A concordance is a useful tool that shows various verses in the Bible where a particular word is used. The value of this tool is that you are able to gain a better understanding of what a word means by seeing how it is used throughout Scripture. A concordance also helps you to find verses when you only remember a portion of a particular verse.

Concordances come in several forms, varying primarily in degree of completeness. Some give only a few verses where a particular word is used, while others give an exhaustive treatment to a word.[2] The less complete ones are quicker to use, while the more exhaustive ones are better for in-depth study. They both have their place. Concordances also vary regarding the translation they are based on. Most of the major concordances are based on King James Version wording, a fact that tends to decrease their effectiveness for those who use another translation of the Bible.

One of the most practical uses of a concordance is for doing word studies. A word study is helpful when seeking a better understanding of the meaning of a word, or when seeking to get a feel for the systematic teachings of the Word of God on certain words. The following illustrates how this can be done:

Step one: List the various references under a word in the concordance on a sheet of paper. Be selective if using an exhaustive concordance.

Step two: Look up each reference and briefly summarize the idea the verse presents regarding the word and write it next to the verse listed on the sheet of paper.

Step three: Group the verses into some basic categories for better understanding. For example, use categories such as who, what, when, where, why, and how to start.

Step four: Summarize findings and list an outline of truths discovered on a new sheet of paper, listing verse references under each item.

If you follow these four steps, you should gain a clear understanding of the biblical emphasis regarding a word. See Figure 11 for examples of this for the words *Spirit* and *flesh* as found in John 3:6 and how such a concordance study would look after step four.

Such word studies will force you to approach your study of God's Word in a synthesizing manner. The method is also quite simple and uncomplicated, so most people will be able to utilize it in their study of God's Word.

The fourth method of studying God's Word in a

synthesizing way is to learn to use a topical Bible. A topical Bible works on the same principle as a concordance, but it references topics instead of words. Thus, using a topical Bible will supplement your marginal referencing of topics, as well as enable you to do general topical studies of the Word of God. A topical Bible is easy to use and often has entire verses written out in the text. I have used them to great advantage in my own ministry and have found the topical Bible to be the most frequently used tool by those with whom I work.

HOLY SPIRIT*

I. Who He is
1. Eternal God (Heb. 9:14)
2. Power of God (Luke 1:35; Rom. 15:19)
3. Spirit of God (John 4:24)
II. Where He is
1. With us (1 Cor. 6:19)
2. Everywhere (Ps. 139:7)
III. What He does
1. Author of new birth (John 3:5,6)
2. Convicts world of sin (John 16:8)
3. Inspires Scripture (2 Tim. 3:16; 2 Peter 1:21)
4. Sanctifies believers (Rom. 15:16)
5. Gives us spiritual gifts (1 Cor. 12:4)
6. Produces fruit in us (Gal. 5:22,23)
7. Gives us understanding (John 14:26)
IV. Symbols of Spirit
1. Water (John 7:38,39)
2. Fire (Acts 2:3)
3. Wind (John 3:8)
4. Oil (1 John 2:27)
5. Dove (Matt. 3:16)
6. Rain (Hos. 6:3)

FLESH*

I. What the flesh is
1. Physical body (Ps. 16:9; Acts 2:26)
2. Old nature (Rom. 7; Gal. 5)
II. What the flesh is like (old nature)
1. Corrupt, sinful (Rom. 7:25)
2. Weak (Matt. 26:41)
3. Wars with Spirit (Gal. 5:16)
4. Cannot please God (Rom. 8:8)
III. Fruits of flesh (2 Cor. 12:20,21; Gal. 5:19–21; Col. 3:5–9)
1. Immorality
2. Impurity
3. Sensuality
4. Idolatry
5. Sorcery
6. Strife
7. Jealousy
8. Anger
9. Envy
10. Gossip

*These are abbreviated, not exhaustive studies.

Fig. 11 Word Studies

CONCLUDING SUGGESTIONS

Let me conclude this chapter by making several suggestions to those who desire to become students of the Word. First, I feel that it is indispensable to follow a plan of devotional study that takes you through the Bible at least once a year. Overview is essential to the proper understanding of God's Word. A growing sense of the totality of Scripture does much to prevent extremes in interpretation. When such a plan is followed consistently and coupled with the development of marginal references, a person cannot help but become more knowledgeable and able to use the Word of God as a tool in effective ministry. Reading approximately three chapters a day should accomplish this goal.

Second, anyone who aspires to be a disciple, and thus a man of the Word, should begin to build a library of basic Bible study aids. Such a library will do much to help develop independence in the life of the Christian you are discipling. The following list would be the minimum that should constitute this library:

> At least three different translations of the Bible
> A good study/reference Bible
> A Bible handbook
> A good concordance
> A Bible dictionary
> A topical Bible
> A good one-volume commentary

Third, a growing disciple should be gaining a knowledge of sound rules for interpreting the Bible. This calls for an understanding of biblical hermeneutics. As I noted in chapter 4, such a topic is beyond the scope of this book. Yet I feel that it is important that Christians gain such an understanding so they are less apt to manipulate God's Word into their preconceived ideas of what it would teach. For several years I have taught the laymen and students with whom I work some of the basic rules of orthodox hermeneutics. A Bible student should know a summary of such rules.

Fourth, I would be remiss if I didn't stress the need for application in this section of Bible study. As I have stressed throughout this book, a disciple is not one who merely hears the truth, but rather one who has become an obedient doer of the Word. It is vital that our focus be on application; there is great danger to Christians in gaining knowledge without application. Three passages of Scripture point out some of these dangers.

1. "Therefore, everyone who hears these words of mine and puts them into practice is like a wise man who built his house on the rock. The rain came down, the streams rose, and the winds blew and beat against that house; yet it did not fall, because it had its foundation on the rock. But everyone who hears these words of mine and does not put them into practice is like a foolish man who built his house on sand. The rain came down, the streams rose, and the winds blew and beat against that house, and it fell with a great crash" (Matt. 7:24–27).

This passage clearly shows that knowledge without application will not yield any stability to a Christian's life. We build on the rock only through application.

2. "When an evil spirit comes out of a man, it goes through arid places seeking rest and does not find it. Then it says, 'I will return to the house I left' " (Luke 11:24).

This passage links blessings from God to application of the Word. There is no blessing for the man whose interest in the Bible is purely academic.

3. "Do not merely listen to the word, and so deceive

yourselves. Do what it says. Anyone who listens to the word but does not do what it says is like a man who looks at his face in a mirror and, after looking at himself, goes away and immediately forgets what he looks like. But the man who looks intently into the perfect law that gives freedom, and continues to do this, not forgetting what he has heard, but doing it — he will be blessed in what he does" (James 2:22–25).

Here we see that those who see the truth yet don't apply it to their lives become self-deceived over time. Without application, we will become hardened to future application and unable to truly sense our condition and need.

I would like to stress that there are no gimmicks for applying God's Word to your life. Application is a product of your disciplined obedience to God's commands and the empowering of the Holy Spirit to carry out your obedience. Yet, although there are no shortcuts to application, there are some things we can do to aid us in the process. The most important help to our application is to clarify the specific areas in our lives which a given portion of the Word speaks to and then lay out a plan, or strategy, to deal with these areas.

To begin to clarify the specific areas that a portion of Scripture speaks to, we should ask ourselves the following questions:

1. In the case of a doctrinal truth:
   - "Does this truth reinforce what I already believed about God, salvation, or another doctrine?"
   - "If not, how does it change my previous beliefs, and does this change affect other areas of my doctrine?"

2. In the case of a command or promise:

- "Does this verse command an activity that I have not been doing?"
- "Does this verse command an attitude I have not been manifesting?"
- "Does this verse point out an area for further study and training for my growth and fruitfulness?"
- "Have I accepted and trusted God for this promise?"

By asking such questions as these, the practical import of a portion of Scripture begins to be seen. We must never be satisfied with less than this perspective.

Next we should develop a plan or strategy to implement the teaching we have found. This second point primarily refers to commands and can be done by following a number of steps.

Step One: Determine possible areas of application.

1. Relationship to God
2. Relationship to family
3. Relationship to Christian friends
4. Relationship to non-Christians

Step Two: Think of the specific ways in which a verse applies to such areas of application.

Step Three: Specify what you can do (in detail) today, this week, and this month to carry out the application.

Step Four: Commit your applications to God in prayer, then step out and obediently do them.

Remember, knowledge without application can be deadening to our Christian lives. Be sure you are a doer, not only a hearer. In order to help your disciple become a doer, you must already be one.

In conclusion, I want to stress once again the importance of simplicity. Unless a method is easy to follow and reasonable in its time demands, few people will follow it consistently. Thus we must balance the ideal with the real.

A simple method is of no value unless it yields valuable results for the user.

Notes

[1]See Kuhne, *Dynamics of Personal Follow-up*, p. 92.

[2]I would suggest spending a couple of hours at your local Christian bookstore examining firsthand the various concordances available.

7

The Relationship of Fellowship to Discipleship Training

If I were to summarize the single most important factor affecting disciple-building that I have learned in my ministry, it would be the role of the fellowship of Christians, the body of Christ, in the effective growth of a new Christian. Recent experiences in my ministry have forcefully confronted me with this issue. I am thus including an examination of the role of the body in disciple-building as part of this book.

The body of believers plays a crucial role in the nurture of new believers. This role of the body is basically twofold. First, the body provides formal and informal instruction for the new believer. Second, the body helps integrate the new Christian into the benefits of the corporate ministry of the body. Let's examine each of these aspects more fully.

Formally, instruction in the faith is achieved through the new-believers classes, sermons, Sunday school, and so on. Much of a person's understanding of his faith grows out of such formal instruction. It is the rare person who is disciplined enough to be totally on his own in studying and growing in knowledge. Since knowledge is necessary for growth, the personal follow-up and discipleship training of a growing Christian must include opportunities to receive the benefits of such corporate offerings.

Informally, the body of believers also provides vital instruction for the growing Christian. One way this is accomplished is through the example of the lives of more mature believers. The fellowship of Christians provides an opportunity to see the practical demonstration of Christian virtues. Such an opportunity is often key in stimulating us to obedience in some area of our lives. The second way the body informally instructs us is through the mutual sharing of what God is doing in each life. To see God answering the prayers of others stimulates us to confident prayers. To see someone learn something significant in his devotions often produces renewed commitment to consistency in this area of our lives. Thus the body is important to the growing Christian because of the formal and informal instruction it provides.

The second important role of the body is to aid the integration of the new believer into the benefits of the corporate ministry of the body. Such an integration is indispensable in achieving all that God has for us in this life. However, becoming a part of the body is not automatic. Although we are positionally baptized into Christ's body (the church) at conversion, the experiential integration does not always happen. Examine Figure 12 on page 147 to see why.

Experientially, the body of believers is made up of a complex web of relationships. The body is a functioning organism resulting from such relationships, and becoming a part of the organism of the body requires more than being around the body. Spatial proximity does not guarantee integration. At a conference where I spoke recently,

I asked those who were recent converts to stand up (recent being defined as within the past two years). I then asked how many went to church consistently, and all said they did. I then asked them to analyze their involvement, and if they felt they were really part of the body at their church to remain standing; if not, to sit down. Everyone sat down!

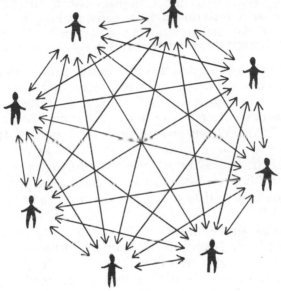

Fig. 12

The only way to become part of the organism of the body is through relationships. Only when those inside the web of the body go out of their way to build relationships with those outside and assist them in establishing additional relationships with others in the web will new Christians be able to become part of the body and benefit from what it can offer. How urgent it is that the church realize its responsibility!

As I have already said, integration into the body is

important because of the corporate benefits of the body ministry. Let's now turn our attention to these benefits and examine why they are important.

1. The first corporate benefit of the body is *protection*.

> See to it, brothers that none of you has a sinful, unbe-lieving heart that turns away from the living God. But encourage one another daily, as long as it is called Today, so that none of you may be hardened by sin's deceitfulness (Heb. 3:12,13).

The body plays an essential role in our protection against the effects of sin. Part of God's provision for us in overcoming sin is to be found within the body. Sin does two things to the Christian, according to this passage. First, sin hard-ens the heart. When we sin and don't deal with it cor-rectly, a slight hardening of heart occurs. This makes us less and less aware of the convicting ministry of the Holy Spirit within us. This increasing hardness produces an increasing probability of further sin and is a serious prob-lem.

Second, sin deceives us. This means that sin makes us increasingly unaware of our true condition. We become cold in our faith and aren't even aware that it is happening. Thus sin comes at us with a two-pronged attack and is dangerous for this reason. If we were totally alone in our Christian walk and the above process began to proceed, our chances of victory would be slim.

The body provides protection for us in this problem. Because of a mutual concern for one another, a Christian who is beginning to grow cold and hard would be no-ticed quickly. The members of the body would rush to his aid by encouraging him to repent and deal with his sin. What a blessing not to be left at the mercy of our own de-ceptions!

I have seen numerous cases where a growing Chris-tian admitted that involvement in the body was the key to his recognizing and dealing with some sin in his life. I feel this is probably the most common reason why those who don't participate in fellowship grow cold in their faith. It isn't that they were uncommitted or undesirous of growth. It is just that without the protection of the body, they inevitably become deceived and hardened. No man is an island unto himself in the Christian life. God never intended us to be outside the benefits of the body.

2. The second corporate benefit of the body is a combination of *encouragement* and *stimulation*.

> And let us consider how we may spur one another on toward love and good deeds. Let us not give up meeting together, as some are in the habit of doing, but let us encourage one another — and all the more as you see the Day approaching (Heb. 10:24,25).

Whereas the first corporate benefit was somewhat negative in emphasis, the second is joyfully positive. Not only does the body provide protection, but it also gives us encouragement and stimulation. The mutual involvement of committed lives is meant to provide a source of motivation for godly living.

The word *stimulate* is the translation of the Greek word *paroxusmos*. This word means to incite, stimulate, or provoke. The body of believers must be attentive to its need to incite one another to ministry and growth. Personally I have found a stimulation to love and good works when I am interacting with other committed believers. If a growing Christian is not in a position where he interacts with other committed believers in the body, his growth will be adversely affected.

Such corporate meeting together is not the normal orientation of the Christian, either now or in the early church. Thus it is necessary to be constantly encouraged, or exhorted, to participate in a meaningful fellowship with one another. The body, when involved in such encouragement of its members, becomes its own self-perpetuator.

3. The third corporate benefit of the body is *meaningful worship experiences.*

> Let the word of Christ dwell in you richly as you teach and counsel one another with all wisdom, and as you sing psalms, hymns and spiritual songs with gratitude in your hearts to God. (Col. 3:16).

Meaningful, joyful worship of God is a product of body ministry. I often hear people say they can worship God better when they are alone. This is simply untrue. Solitude may stimulate meditation upon God, but it is never the key to worship. Worship is meant to be a corporate activity. The sharing of praises, songs, thanksgivings, and prayers are the keys to worship.

This principle is seen throughout the Old Testament as well as the New. To be in a multitude of people who are praising God stimulates us to worship Him as well. The new Christian who misses out on the corporate worship of God will certainly be negatively affected. In my previous campus ministry, I found that one of the most important elements in stimulating the commitment of various Christians was their participation in our corporate times of worship. To be able to praise God is a blessing we all were meant to experience.

4. The fourth corporate benefit of the body is the *sharing of needs.*

> Carry each other's burdens, and in this way you will fulfill the law of Christ (Gal. 6:2).

The fourth corporate benefit of the body is that we can rest in the concern of others. We are not alone in our problems, and the body will seek to meet our needs. To be able to share with others our sorrows and our burdens is a blessed privilege. To know others are concerned about our needs is reassuring to the suffering saint. God intends this to be a source of comfort for us, just as He Himself is a comfort in times of trials.

The clear picture in the New Testament is the seriousness with which the early church accepted their responsibilities to one another. From the communal living in the Book of Acts through the contributions to widows and brethren facing famine, the sharing of needs is seen. This type of sharing gives a practical picture to the growing believers of what it means to be walking in love. This picture is achieved no other way.

5. The fifth corporate benefit of the body is *mutual prayer*.

> They devoted themselves to the apostles' teaching and to the fellowship, to the breaking of bread and to prayer (Acts 2:42).

The Book of Acts focuses often on the role of prayer. The church was found praying in times of persecution, for physical provisions, for missions, etc. Every need was brought before the body for corporate prayer. The Epistles also clearly stress this important function of the body. In addition to being a function, it was also a benefit.

We have found that when the body prays together over specific needs, the answers are a shared blessing. Many new Christians have shared with me the excitement they feel when they see such definite proofs of God's concern and activity. The corporate prayer often provides the mutual stimulation necessary for consistency in personal prayer life, another benefit for the growing believer.

There are other corporate benefits of the body of believers, but the previous five are essential to understand the necessity of the body in the effective personal follow-up and discipleship training of new believers. These benefits are to be found nowhere else.

I must admit, however, that the body does not always act in the way God intends it to act. A body of believers might not be performing any of the above functions. I feel that if we are involved in such a dead body, that we must do something to provide an alternative to new Christians. The above body ministries are not dependent on a building but rather upon the mutual commitment to one another of a body of believers. Regardless of size, when this commitment exists, a body becomes a functioning church, at least in its ability to achieve the five benefits identified.

You really have no option but to provide such a body ministry. This is indispensable to your ministry, but more importantly, it is indispensable to yourself.

Structuring
Discipling Mi

This final chapter focuses on how to carry out specifically the instruction involved in building a Christian in discipleship training. Personal follow-up of a new believer is a structured period of teaching and takes between twelve to fifteen weeks to accomplish. At the end of this period of ministry you should be able to determine whom to continue to minister to in a disciple-building work. It is important to have some direction in the discipleship-training process when continuing to work with someone beyond personal follow-up.

The dividing line between personal study and one-to-one ministry is not as sharp in discipleship training as it is in personal follow-up. In fact, a large portion of the one-to-one ministry in discipleship training is simply reviewing the personal study of the growing disciple and answering questions associated with it. Although one-to-one work also involves counseling, problem solving, and helping to achieve personal application of the Word of

153

he life of the growing disciple, the supervision of
rsonal study gives direction and ongoing purpose to
r meeting together.

This section focuses on the personal study of the new believer, analyzing the *what* and *when* in discipleship training. Let me summarize the topics I feel are essential to cover in a total follow-up program (including those necessary for discipleship training). The following topics are divided into three category areas.

DEVOTIONAL AREA:

1. Salvation	6. Bible study methods	11. Discipline
2. Assurance	7. Confession	12. Habits
3. Devotions	8. Dealing with temptation	13. Guidance
4. Prayer	9. Holy Spirit	14. Stewardship
5. Memory	10. Obedience	15. Church

DOCTRINAL AREA:

1. Bible doctrine	3. Apologetics
2. Systematic Bible knowledge	4. Counseling

DISCIPLESHIP AREA:

1. Evangelism	4. Counseling
2. Testimony	5. Apologetics
3. Follow-up	6. Time management

A number of these topics are covered during the personal follow-up stage with the growing disciple. All the topics should be covered or reviewed during the discipleship-training stage.

I would now like to suggest how to schedule the whole period of personal study in discipleship training. Your role is to keep reviewing and sharing with the growing disciple to make sure that he is reading, understanding, and applying the data. I will assume that the discipleship training begins in the twelfth week of personal ministry (or after approximately three months).[1] The following is a suggested guide for combining one-to-one ministry with supervised personal study to give a definite direction to your discipleship-training ministry. The weeks are only approximations and the period of study could easily cover two years of time.

Weeks 12 - 18: Study on Spiritual Growth

A. Assign one of the following books to be read, and review it chapter by chapter:
   1. Watchman Nee, *The Normal Christian Life* (Fort Washington, Pa. Christian Literature Crusade, 1961).
   2. Fritz Ridenour, *How to Be a Christian Without Being Religious* (Glendale, Calif.: Regal, 1967).
   3. Francis Schaeffer, *True Spirituality* (Wheaton, Ill.: Tyndale, 1971).
B. Begin the study of transferable concepts by Bill Bright of Campus Crusade for Christ as the structure for devotions. This should take from five to eight weeks. Such things as guidance, confession, obedience, etc., are covered in these concepts.
C. Get the Christian started in a Bible memory program. This memorization should continue throughout his discipleship training (and beyond). Review his progress week by week. The following are good programs to follow:
   1. Topical Memory System (Navigators)
   2. Bible Memory Course (Campus Crusade for Christ, International)

Weeks 19 - 25: Ministry Skills — Evangelism

A. Train the new Christian to share his faith in a clear, practical way. Using a prepared booklet is a great help in achieving this. The following booklets are easy to learn and use, and have proven effective in evangelism. Choose one and train him.
   1. *Steps to Peace With God,* by Billy Graham
   2. *Bridge to Life* (Navigators)

      3. *The Four Spiritual Laws,* by Bill Bright (Campus Crusade for Christ, International)

B. Help the Christian refine his evangelistic testimony. (See Appointment IX in the follow-up series in *Dynamics of Personal Follow-up,* pp. 194–200.)

C. Assign one of the following books to be read, and review it chapter by chapter:
      1. Leroy Eims, *Winning Ways* (Wheaton, Ill.: Victor, 1974).
      2. Paul Little, *How to Give Away Your Faith* (Downers Grove, Ill.: InterVarsity Press, 1966).

Weeks 26 - 32: Basic Doctrine

A. Assign the growing disciple to begin to work through Francis Schaeffer's *Basic Bible Studies* (Wheaton: Tyndale, 1973) in his devotions. This will take him six to eight weeks.

B. Assign one of the following books to be read, and review it chapter by chapter:
      1. Paul Little, *Know What you Believe* (Downers Grove, Ill.: InterVarsity Press, 1968).
      2. John Stott, *Basic Christianity* (Grand Rapids: Eerdmans, 1958).

C. Encourage the disciple to attend a class on basic doctrine at a local church or Bible college. If this is not possible, seek to enroll him in a correspondence study program through a Bible institute or college.

Weeks 33 - 40: Overview of the Bible

A. Assign the following books to be read, and review them chapter by chapter to aid the growing disciple to have an overview of the Bible's contents:
E.T.T.A. Series on Bible Survey:
Old Testament — Law and History

Old Testament — Poetry and Prophecy
New Testament Survey
(These textbooks are available from the Evangelical Teacher Training Association, 499 Gunderson Drive, Box 327, Wheaton, Ill. 60187.)

B. Encourage him to buy a Bible handbook and begin to use it as an aid in his study of the Bible. The following are possible choices:
   1. *Halley's Bible Handbook* (Grand Rapids: Zondervan, 1965).
   2. *Unger's Bible Handbook* (Chicago: Moody Press, 1966).
C. He should understand the concept of inspiration of the Scriptures. Be sure to develop this concept for him.

Weeks 41 - 48: Practical Apologetics

A. Assign the following books to be read to aid the growing disciple in making a defense of his faith and in answering common questions that come up. Review the points.
   1. C. S. Lewis, *Mere Christianity* (New York: Macmillan, 1960).
   2. Paul Little, *Know Why You Believe* (Downers Grove, Ill.: InterVarsity Press, 1968).
B. Encourage him to buy the following books for reference tools in his ministry:
   1. Josh McDowell, *Evidence That Demands a Verdict* (Arrowhead Springs, Calif.: Campus Crusade for Christ, 1972).
   2. Bernard Ramm, *Protestant Christian Evidences* (Chicago: Moody Press, 1953).
C. Because dealing with the cults, or at least understanding what they teach, is an important area of apologetics, one of the following books would be a helpful reference tool for the growing disciple. It is

not necessary to assign reading in this area unless a problem arises with cults.

1. Ronald Enroth, *Youth, Brainwashing and the Extremist Cults* (Zondervan, 1977).
2. Walter Martin, *Kingdom of the Cults* (Bethany Fellowship, 1968).
3. Fritz Ridenour, *So What's the Difference?* (Regel, 1967).

Weeks 49 - 55: Bible Study Methods

Seek to train the growing disciple in the methods developed in chapter 6. This should take six weeks.

Weeks 56 - 64: Ministry Skills — Follow-up

A. Every growing disciple should understand the importance of a personal follow-up ministry. Assign my book *The Dynamics of Personal Follow-up*, reviewing the chapters and assisting him in learning the follow-up appointments. Encourage him to begin follow-up of a new Christian.
B. Encourage the reading of the following books:
   1. Robert Coleman, *The Master Plan of Evangelism* (Revell, 1963).
   2. Walter Henrichsen, *Disciples Are Made, Not Born* (Wheaton, Ill.: Victor, 1974).

Weeks 65 - 75: Philosophical Apologetics

A. Assign and review the trilogy of books by Francis Schaeffer on our culture with the aid of a fourth book, *Introduction to Fancis Schaeffer* (IVP, 1974). The trilogy of books are:
   The God Who Is There (IVP, 1968).
   He Is There and He Is Not Silent (Tyndale, 1972).
   Escape From Reason (IVP, 1968).
B. This study will take at least six weeks, probably more.

Weeks 76 - 84: Ministry Skills — Counseling

A. It is important that the growing disciple know how to use the Bible to solve problems. The following books by Jay Adams are excellent for this purpose:
   1. *Competent to Counsel* (Grand Rapids: Baker, 1972).
   2. *The Use of the Scriptures in Counseling* (Grand Rapids: Baker, 1975).
B. Encourage discussion of problems and work together toward biblical solutions.

An added program of study could be geared to transferability on the part of the growing disciple. Probably the best way to accomplish this is to have the disciple develop seminars on the topics he is studying, and then give him opportunities to use them in Sunday school classes, group studies, or retreats. The following is an example of such a program of guided study I have used successfully with students and laymen. It has taken an average of six to eight months for the disciple to complete each study, especially when most of the books were previously read during the guided personal study period.

GUIDED STUDY COURSE

Part 1. Evangelism

A. Read:
   1. *Winning Ways*, by Leroy Eims
   2. *How to Give Away Your Faith*, by Paul Little
   3. *Say It With Love*, by Howard Hendricks
   4. *Sharing God's Love*, by Rosalind Rinker (Grand Rapids: Zondervan, 1976).
B. Prepare:
   1. From your reading in Part A, develop a seminar on one of the following topics:
      a. Pre-evangelism strategy

      b. Friendship evangelism
      c. Opening conversations, or moving existing ones to evangelism
      d. Your choice

Part 2. Follow-up/Discipleship

A. Read:
1. *Disciples Are Made, Not Born*, by Walter Henrichsen
2. *The Dynamics of Discipleship Training*, by Gary Kuhne
3. *The Dynamics of Personal Follow-up*, by Gary Kuhne
4. *Master Plan of Evangelism*, by Robert Coleman
5. *New Testament Follow-up*, by Waylon Moore

B. Prepare:
1. A seminar on what it means to be a disciple
2. A seminar on what you consider to be key factors in disciple-building.

Part 3. Apologetics

A. Read:
1. *Know Why You Believe*, by Paul Little
2. *Evidence that Demands a Verdict*, by Josh McDowell
3. *Mere Christianity*, by C. S. Lewis
4. Trilogy by Francis Schaeffer (Use study guide)
5. *Dust of Death*, by Os Guinness (Downers Grove, Ill.: InterVarsity Press, 1973).

B. Prepare:
1. A seminar on some point in traditional apologetics, i.e., inspiration, the Resurrection, etc.
2. A seminar on some point in philosophical apologetics, i.e., absolutes, culture, etc.

Part 4. Body Life
A. Read:
1. *Body Life*, by Ray Stedman
2. *New Face for the Church*, by Lawrence O. Richards (Grand Rapids: Zondervan, 1970).
3. *Becoming One in the Spirit*, by Lawrence O. Richards (Wheaton, Ill.: Victor, 1973).
4. *Reciprocal Living*, W. I. M.

B. Prepare:
1. A biblical study on topic of unity and mutual ministry.
2. Do a seminar on the topic of becoming one in the Spirit.

Part 5. Biblical Overview
A. Read:
1. *The New Testament Speaks*, by Glenn W. Barker et al. (New York: Harper & Row, 1969).
2. *The Old Testament Speaks*, by Samuel J. Schultz (New York: Harper & Row, 1970).
3. *New Testament Times*, by Merrill C. Tenney (Grand Rapids: Eerdmans, 1965).

B. Prepare:
1. An outline showing the major emphasis of each book of the New Testament.
2. A seminar on the culture of the New Testament period.

Part 6. Spirit-filled Living
A. Read:
1. *He That Is Spiritual*, by Lewis Sperry Chafer
2. *True Spirituality*, by Francis Schaeffer
3. *The Normal Christian Life*, by Watchman Nee
4. *The Christian's Secret of a Happy Life*, by Hannah Whitall Smith (Old Tappan, N.J.: Revell, 1968).

161

The Dynamics of Discipleship Training

B. Prepare a seminar on what it means to grow in Christ, i.e., why, how, when, etc.

This then is the direction that discipleship training would normally follow over a period ranging from one and one-half to two years. Let me emphasize again that the dividing line between personal study and one-to-one ministry is not sharp in discipleship training. By following this system of guided review of personal study, you will accomplish two things. First, you will have a definite direction in your ministry and a legitimate purpose for meeting together weekly with the growing disciple. Second, as a result of this consistent meeting together, you will be able to counsel the growing disciple in his problems and truly transfer your life into another. Remember that this chapter is a *suggestion*, not a strait jacket.

May God use these directions and this book to enable you to accomplish His program of discipleship training, thus allowing you the privilege of spiritual reproduction.

Notes

[1]The first ten weeks (of personal follow-up) are found in Kuhne, *Dynamics of Personal Follow-up*, pp. 145–207. Because of missed appointments or other variables, the author has provided an extra week between follow-up and discipleship training.